W9-CAS-275

Knitty
Gritty
Knits

Knitty Gritty Knits

25 Fun & Fabulous Projects

Vickie Howell

LARK BOOKS

A Division of Sterling Publishing Co., Inc.
New York

Series Editor:	Dawn Cusick
Series Designer:	Thom Gaines
Cover Designer:	DIY Network, Stewart Pack
Technical Editor:	Laura Polley
Assistant Editor:	Matt Paden
Contributing Writer:	Jane Laferla
Production:	Charlie Covington
Illustrator:	Orrin Lundgren

10 9 8 7 6 5 4 3 2 1

First Edition

Published by Lark Books, A Division of
Sterling Publishing Co., Inc.
387 Park Avenue South, New York, N.Y. 10016

Text © 2006, Lark Books
Photography © 2006, DIY Network
Illustrations © 2006, Lark Books

Distributed in Canada by Sterling Publishing,
c/o Canadian Manda Group, 165 Dufferin Street
Toronto, Ontario, Canada M6K 3H6

Distributed in the United Kingdom by GMC Distribution Services,
Castle Place, 166 High Street, Lewes, East Sussex, England BN7 1XU

Distributed in Australia by Capricorn Link (Australia) Pty Ltd.,
P.O. Box 704, Windsor, NSW 2756 Australia

The written instructions, photographs, designs, patterns, and projects in this volume are intended for the personal use of the reader and may be reproduced for that purpose only. Any other use, especially commercial use, is forbidden under law without written permission of the copyright holder.

Every effort has been made to ensure that all the information in this book is accurate. However, due to differing conditions, tools, and individual skills, the publisher cannot be responsible for any injuries, losses, and other damages that may result from the use of the information in this book.

If you have questions or comments about this book, please contact:

Lark Books
67 Broadway
Asheville, NC 28801
(828) 253-0467

Manufactured in China

All rights reserved

ISBN 13: 978-1-57990-916-1
ISBN 10: 1-57990-916-7

For information about custom editions, special sales, premium and corporate purchases, please contact Sterling Special Sales Department at 800-805-5489 or specialsales@sterlingpub.com.

Contents

I grew up in a crafty family. My mom had me making things as soon as I was old enough to hold the tools on my own. I've embroidered, needlepointed, crocheted, sewed, latch hooked, painted, decoupaged, punch embroidered, glued, glittered, and bejeweled as long as I can remember.

My mom tried teaching me to knit when I was eight, but I hated it. I like to blame my young distaste for the knit on the abrasive, acrylic yarns and aluminum needles that were common in the 1970s. (Perhaps I was a yarn snob even then!) Looking back on it, though, I think that my little hands just had trouble maneuvering both the needles and the yarn, and in those days, if I didn't pick up on something right away, I moved on to the next craft.

I didn't think about knitting again until I was in my 20s. It took a friend a solid year of hassling me to get me to go to her favorite yarn store. As soon as I walked through the door and saw the endless possibilities of color, textures, and materials, I fell head over needles! I started knitting that day and haven't stopped since. To this day, I'm powerless against beautiful yarns.

The shop owner helped me with my knitting, and my mom was also on call for those late nights when I'd drop a stitch or make some other random mistake. I would literally get in my car, in my pj's, and drive over to her house so she could fix it right away. I guess I was, and remain to this day, a little obsessed.

Since I was pregnant with one of my sons when I picked up knitting, my earliest projects were all about baby. Later though, I wrote *New Knits on the Block,* a collection of toys, costumes, and play things in response to my kids' lackluster reaction to traditional items such as socks and mittens I had made for them in the past.

Knitty Gritty Knits

Perhaps that was the beginning of *Knitty Gritty* style. If I had to define the *Knitty Gritty* style, I'd say it's all about infusing a traditional, old-world craft with a modern, funkier outlook—taking the craft and giving it a quirky, creative twist. I like to add just a touch of edge to my projects, and I'm inspired by music, movies, pop-culture, and fashion history.

My show on DIY Network has been a dream come true. In this cookie-cutter culture we live in, I firmly believe that positive self-expression is crucial. DIY Network's arts and crafts shows encourage such expression. I love the fact that, in the large forum of television, knitting can be just as accessible to the urban art kid as well as the midwestern grandmother. I have been thrilled by the amount of positive feedback that I've gotten from *Knitty Gritty* viewers. I love my TV Land Knitsters!

To me, knitting is more than just the act of putting yarn to needle. It represents creative expression (through choosing colors and fibers), history (through the creation of heirlooms), community (through both live and virtual knitting groups), and stress reduction and relaxation (through rhythmic movement). But it's also fun, hip, and expressive of the creative edge that's in every one of us. And that's exactly what I hope you will find in the pages of this book.

Vickie Howell,
Host of DIY Network's *Knitty Gritty*

Knitty Gritty Knits

diy network

1

Knitting Basics

This chapter is guaranteed to help you get your *Knitty Gritty* groove on. Even if you don't know knit from purl, you'll find all the basic information you will need to make the projects in this book. From navigating needles to substituting yarns for great results, from cast ons to bind offs and all the stitches in between, you're just a few steps away from making that great piece you've been dreaming about. So grab your needles, choose your yarns, and get knitting!

YARN

Yarns are made from nearly every kind of material these days—from animal or plant fibers to synthetics and metals. Animal fibers include wool, mohair, alpaca, angora, and even possum, while plant fibers include cotton, linen, and hemp. Blends combine the softness and warmth of natural fibers with the unique properties of synthetics. An acrylic/wool-blend yarn, for example, will have the drape and insulation of a wool fiber, along with the easy-care advantages of acrylic.

Yarns are spun in various ways to achieve a particular effect, giving the knitted fabric a distinctive look. For example, yarn may be very smooth and flat, or be deliberately overtwisted in places to create a loopy, boucle look. Very fine yarns make for small stitches and slower knitting, but they are perfect for lace patterns or delicate garments. Heavier yarns range from worsted (medium) weight all the

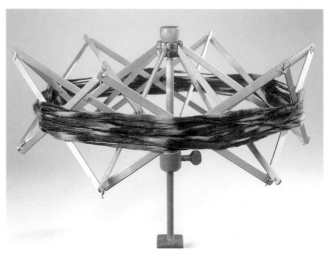

Umbrella swift

way up to superbulky, lending warmth to sweaters and outerwear, and knitting up much more quickly. Novelty yarns often sport a highly textured look or a unique combination of fibers. These yarns are very popular with beginning knitters, because their texture fills in gaps caused by uneven stitches, and because they can achieve great visual interest using only the plainest of stitch patterns.

Knitting yarns come in many different "put-ups," or packaging styles. They may look like round balls, long skeins, or twisted hanks, and they may also be sold in cones. Always buy enough yarn of the same dye lot to complete your project, as the yarn shop may run out quickly. Dye lot is the key to uniform coloration of your knitting: though two dye lots may appear identical to the eye, they will knit up with obvious color differences. Leftover balls of yarn can be returned to your shop, or you can keep them in your stash for use in multicolor projects.

The labels found on commercially produced yarns provide a great deal of information. They'll tell you the exact fiber content and a typical knitting gauge for that yarn. Suggested needle sizes are usually given, as well as care instructions for the particular yarn.

WINDING YARNS

Many yarns today need to be rewound into a ball before you begin to knit. To do this, lay the hank around a chair back, or a skein in a deep shoe box. Beginning at one end of the yarn, wind into a ball until the entire ball is ready to use. Commercial ball winders create yarn "cakes," allowing the yarn to be pulled from the center, and are usually used with umbrella swifts, which function in the same way as a chair back to hold the yarn. No matter which method you choose, always keep the tension of the yarn loose as you wind it. Yarn stretches easily and may produce a different gauge if wound too tightly.

SUBSTITUTING YARNS

Ideally, we'd all like to pick out a pattern and have the yarn it specifies readily available, but often this isn't the case. Experienced knitters know that some yarns may be available for only a short time. Even if you are able to find the yarn called for in the pattern, you still might want to use a different one. Perhaps you're allergic to wool yarn, for example, or the cost of the yarn is an important consideration for you. Maybe you're concerned with future care of the garment. For some knitters (and some recipients of knitwear!), the ability to machine-wash an item is crucial. If this applies to you, you'll want to substitute a synthetic or machine-washable blend of fibers.

Whatever your reasons for making a yarn substitution, doing so is not difficult or adventurous, provided you follow this easy process.

First, study the pattern. What is it that appeals to you? Frequently, color is the first thing you'll notice. Or is it the texture? A design detail? Or the shape? Then, make sure the color, fiber, and texture of your substitution yarn will closely match what attracted you to the design in the first place. You can do that by considering a couple of factors.

Study the manufacturer's label. Look at the yardage (meters). This will tell you much of what you need to know. Look at the recommended gauge.

If your pattern calls for 5 sts to the inch (2.5 cm), and the ball band says the yarn knits to an ideal gauge of only 3 sts to the inch (2.5 cm), you can see at once that you might be getting into trouble.

Examine the texture. Feel the "hand" of your proposed substitute yarn. Does the original design have a soft drape? How does the drape of your substitute compare? What structural features does the original yarn have, and how well does your chosen yarn mimic these?

If you're not sure of your choice, or if the substitute yarn is expensive, buy one ball and put it to the test. Even if you decide not to use that yarn after all, you can still find uses for it later, and you'll gain experience with different yarns. You may be able to find small swatches of yarns you're interested in on display for customers. Handle these, and ask if there may be a tiny scrap of the yarn left over for you to test.

Finally, do bear in mind that the finished article will not look exactly the same when you substitute a yarn. If you make an informed choice, though, you're likely to be pleased with the results. You may even like the project better, knowing that you've taken some control of your choices!

YARN TYPES AND TEXTURES

There are so many fun yarns on today's market, just looking at them inspires new ideas! Try as many as you can—that's the fun of being a knitter!

◣ BOUCLE ◢

A bumpy-textured yarn made by plying two or more strands of yarn together so that they create little loops along the yarn's surface.

◣ CHENILLE ◢

A soft, fuzzy-textured yarn made by plying strands of thread together with many small strands caught perpendicular to the yarn so that they tuft out. "Chenille" means "caterpillar" in French, and that's what these yarns look and feel like.

◣ MOHAIR ◢

An airy, hairy yarn from the Angora goat. Blends that resemble mohair are called mohair-type yarn. Mohair is known for its "halo," a cloud of fuzz that fills in stitches, making this yarn great for quick knitting without bulk.

◣ PLY ◢

The number of strands twisted together to make the finished yarn.

Boucle

Mohair

4-Ply

Yarn Weights

Weight	Usually Called	Description	Gauge
Superfine	Sock, fingering, laceweight	Thread or very thin yarn	27-32 sts = 4"
Fine	Sport, baby yarn	Traditionally used for baby items and thicker socks.	23-26 sts = 4"
Light	DK, light worsted	Between sport-weight and worsted-weight, relatively new in the U.S., though common in the UK.	21-24 sts = 4"
Medium	Worsted, afghan, Aran	About ⅛ inch (3 mm) thick, this is the most familiar yarn size.	16-20 sts = 4"
Bulky	Chunky, craft, rug yarn	A thick yarn, quick to knit	12-15 sts = 4"
Superbulky	Bulky, roving	A very thick yarn, ¼ inch (6mm) or more in diameter	6-11 sts = 4"

Slub

Variegated

◣ SLUB ◢

A thick bump or "tuft" poking up at intervals along a strand, made by spinning the yarn more loosely at that point, and/or by having more fiber at that point. This is now a popular design element in many yarns, including the yarns otherwise known as "thick & thins."

◣ SPACE-DYED ◢

A multicolored yarn that has been dyed by pouring colors over long spaces along the yarn hank.

◣ VARIEGATED ◢

A multicolor yarn dyed in such a way that regular repeats of the color pattern occur. If dyed by hand, a more random effect may be apparent.

Space-Dyed

TOOLS & SUPPLIES

NEEDLES

Knitting needles come in three basic types—circular, straight, and double-pointed—and are made from a variety of materials. When choosing needles for your own knitting, remember that there is no one "correct" type of needle. No two knitters are the same, so experiment until you know what your needle preferences are, and then go with whatever needles feel the best in your hands!

An assortment
of needles

OTHER TOOLS

- needle gauge
- small pair of scissors or snips
- tapestry needle for sewing up seams
  (these have large eyes and blunt tips)
- blocking pins
- tape measure
- stitch holders
- stitch markers
- cable needle
- notebook and pen

The right tools make the knitting process more fun and gives better results.

KNITTING NEEDLE SIZES

Metric	U.S. Size
2.25mm	1
2.75mm	2
3.25mm	3
3.50mm	4
3.75mm	5
4.00mm	6
4.50mm	7
5.00mm	8
5.50mm	9
6.00mm	10
6.50mm	10½
8.00mm	11
9.00mm	13
10.00mm	15
12.75mm	17
15.00mm	19
19.00mm	35
25.00mm	50

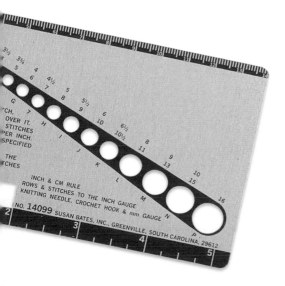

TECHNIQUES

USING PATTERNS AND SCHEMATICS

Before you begin a project, it's a good idea to read through the pattern instructions carefully to familiarize yourself with what you'll be doing.

Pattern instructions are usually given in a range of sizes. Determine which size you want to use, and mark it in some way to highlight your requirements. (If you don't want to mark the pattern itself, photocopy it, then mark it up. Photocopies are also useful so you don't have to carry the whole book around with you.) To determine your size, check the measurements given for the garment.

Remember that even if your bust measurement is 34 inches (86 cm), the finished garment is unlikely to measure 34 inches (86 cm), unless you're knitting a second skin. Almost all patterns have ease added to them. This extra width, which often surprises new knitters, provides wearing comfort. Measure your favorite loose-fitting sweater, and you'll likely find that it actually measures quite a bit more than you are accustomed to thinking of as your "size."

It's a good idea to keep a record of any changes you make in case you want to knit the item again later. You should also note what gauge you achieve with a particular yarn and particular needle size, for future reference.

MAKING AND MEASURING A GAUGE SWATCH

This preparation step is the most important step you can take to ensure good results. Don't skip this step unless you enjoy unpleasant surprises. Making a gauge swatch is a lot like test-driving a car: You need to see how the yarn behaves, how it feels in your hands, and what results you can expect from it. You may even want to wash and dry the swatch to test for shrinkage or

Note the striking difference in gauge caused by switching needle sizes.

color-fastness. Some stitch patterns, like ribbing, pull in widthwise more than you'd think, while others, like lace, can be stretched easily to a much larger width after they're knitted. Once you've selected the yarn and needles, cast on a minimum of 4 inches' (10 cm) worth of stitches, and knit in the stitch pattern called for, to a length of at least 4 inches (10 cm).

Before you measure it, handle the fabric to decide if it feels good enough against the skin to wear comfortably. Does it have the right "hand" for the item you're making? Wash and dry your gauge swatch in the same manner as you plan to wash and dry the finished item. Then, lay your swatch down on a flat surface and place pins to indicate where you'll start measuring. Measure with a ruler, carefully counting the stitches and rows in exactly 4 inches (10 cm). A clear plastic ruler can be very helpful.

As you measure, take care not to stretch the knitting. Also, do not include the edge stitches, which easily distort. If your gauge differs from that given in your pattern by even a fraction of an inch, your finished piece may be significantly larger or smaller than you'd like, which can really be demoralizing. If you have too many stitches per inch, try a larger needle. If you have two few stitches per inch, try a size or two smaller.

TIPS | DIY Network Crafts

What size needle should I use?

If you find yourself with a ball of yarn and you aren't sure which needle size to knit with, grab your needle gauge, double your yarn, and thread it through the closest size hole on the gauge. Whichever hole it fits through best—neither too tight nor with gaping spaces around the yarn—is the best needle size to create your first swatch with.

COMMON ABBREVIATIONS

Review the abbreviations in your pattern instructions to make sure you understand them. If you're unsure about a particular technique, refer to a basic knitting text or ask a knitting buddy to explain it to you.

*	repeat from * as many times as indicated
()	alternate measurement(s)/ stitch counts
alt	alternate
approx	approximately
beg	begin or beginning
bet	between
bl	back loop
BO	bind off
CC	contrast color
cm	centimeter(s)
CO	cast on
cont	continued or continuing
dec	decrease or decreasing
dpn	double-pointed needles
fl	front loop
foll	follow(ing)
g	gram(s)
g st	garter stitch
inc	increase or increasing
k	knit

k2tog	knit two sts together
kwise	knitwise
LH ndl	left hand needle
lp(s)	loops
m	meter(s)
M1	make one (an increase): insert tip of RH needle from front to back under horizontal bar between st just worked and next st on LH needle. Place this loop onto LH needle without twisting it and knit into back of this loop. (One stitch made)
MC	main color
meas	measure
mm	millimeter(s)
ndl	needle
oz	ounces
patt	pattern
p	purl
p2tog	purl 2 together
pm	place marker
psso	pass slipped stitch over
pwise	purlwise

rem	remain or remaining
rev st st	reverse stockinette stitch
RH ndl	right hand needle
rnd(s)	round(s)
RS	right side(s)
SC	single crochet
sk	sklp
sl	slip
ssk	slip 1 st as if to knit, slip 1 st as if to knit, then insert left needle into the front of the two slipped stitches and knit these two sts tog tbl
st(s)	stitch(es)
St st	stockinette stitch
tbl	through the back of loop(s)
tog	together
WS	wrong side(s)
wyib	with yarn in back
wyif	with yarn in front
yd(s)	yards
yo	yarn over
yfd	yarn forward
yrn	yarn round needle

KNIT

Knit and purl are the two stitches on which all other stitches are based. Here's a refresher on the basics of each.

1 Position the yarn at the back of your work. Insert the right needle from front to back into the first stitch on the left needle.

2 Pass the yarn under and then over the right needle. Draw this loop of yarn, and the right needle, back through the stitch you first went into.

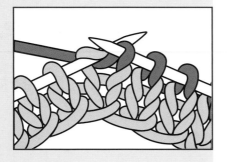

3 Drop the stitch from the left needle. The stitch on the right needle is your knit stitch.

BASIC STITCHES

◢ CASTING ON ◣

Casting on places the first loops on the needle and creates a foundation row for your knitting. There are many ways to cast on, and knitters soon develop favorites. Two popular methods are the single and cable cast ons.

◢ SINGLE CAST ON ◣

1 Make a slip knot on the right needle. Wrap the yarn around your left thumb and secure it with your fingers.

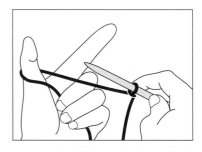

2 Insert needle under the strand on the front of your thumb.

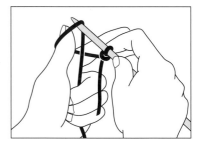

3 Slip this loop onto the needle and pull the yarn to tighten the loop. Repeat this process until you have the desired number of stitches.

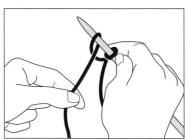

PURL

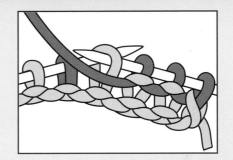

CABLE CAST ON

1 Place a slipknot onto the left needle, and knit one stitch into it. Place the stitch on the left needle. Next, insert the right needle between these two stitches, knit a stitch through this space, and place the stitch back on the left needle.

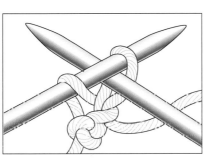

2 Repeat this process until you have the desired number of stitches.

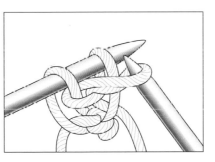

3 This cast on creates a firm edge with the look of a tiny cable, but it is not very elastic. This is a good cast on to use when you must add several stitches at the beginning of a row of knitting.

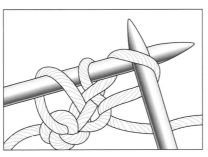

1 Position the yarn at the front of your work. Insert the right needle from back to front into the first stitch on the left needle.

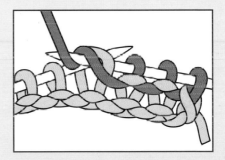

2 Pass the yarn over the right needle from right to left. Draw this loop of yarn, and the right needle, back through the stitch you first went into.

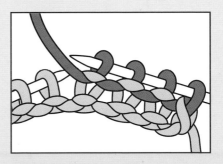

3 Drop the stitch from the left needle. The stitch on the right is your purl stitch.

STOCKINETTE STITCH

This pattern, also called "jersey stitch" or "stocking stitch," is formed on straight needles by knitting and purling alternate rows. Stockinette stitch does not lie flat, but curls on all edges. This can make for an attractive rolled edging for garments, but it can also cause problems when a flat edge is desired. For this reason, most stockinette patterns call for a border of ribbing, moss stitch, or another flat stitch. Traditionally, the "knit" side of stockinette stitch is the right side, but this is not set in stone. If you're using a highly textured yarn, for example, the "wrong" or purl side can often be more attractive, since bumps and loops tend to gravitate toward the purl side. When you use the purl side of the stockinette stitch as the right side, the pattern you create is called reverse stockinette.

GARTER STITCH

This stitch involves no purling! For garter stitch on straight needles, just knit every row. For every two rows you knit, you create one garter "ridge," which makes counting rows a snap. In addition to its neat square proportions, garter stitch is also fully reversible and lies completely flat, making it a perennial favorite even among expert knitters.

CIRCULAR KNITTING

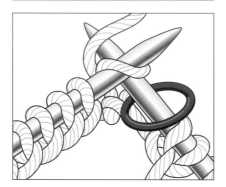

Knitting around in a circle, a technique used most often for socks and sweater yokes, produces a seamless tube of knitted fabric. You can achieve such a tube by using either a circular needle or a set of double pointed needles. (You may see instructions telling you to change from a circular needle to a set of double points when the number of stitches becomes too small to fit around the circular needle.) Circular knitting has incredible advantages, and often results in a garment that is totally seamless! Just cast the stitches onto the circular needle in the usual way, and then join them into a round, making sure that the stitches aren't twisted on the needle. Place a stitch marker or loop of yarn between the first and the last stitch.

Then, using the right-hand needle, knit the first stitch off the left-hand needle, pulling the stitches tightly together at the beginning of the round. Knit around and around, slipping the marker from the left to the right needle each time you come to it. One of the beautiful things about circular

knitting is that the right side is always facing you—this means you can create stockinette stitch without purling at all!

BASIC BIND OFF

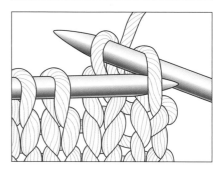

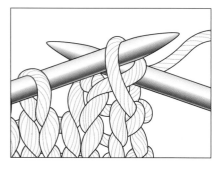

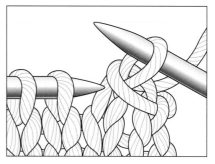

Binding off secures your last row of knitting and allows you to remove it from the needles.

Work the first two stitches on the left-hand needle, then use the point of the left-hand needle to lift the first worked stitch on the right-hand needle over the second worked stitch and off the right needle.

Knit the next stitch on the left-hand needle, and repeat the procedure. To avoid pulling stitches too tightly, keep a tension somewhat looser than the one used for the knitting (it helps to use a needle one or two sizes larger when working the bind-off row.) Stitches are usually bound off in the pattern stitch. For example, in k1p1 rib, you would knit and purl the stitches as they present themselves. When only one stitch remains, break the yarn and pull the resulting tail through the last stitch, tightening to secure.

◣ THREE-NEEDLE BIND OFF ◢

This time-saving technique lets you bind off and join pieces simultaneously. It creates a less bulky seam with a very neat appearance, and is often used for shoulder seams. Just as its name suggests, you use three needles. Arrange the two sets of stitches on the needles, with the right sides together and the wrong sides facing you, and bind off with a needle one or two sizes larger. The bind-off is worked in the usual way, except that you insert the needle into the first stitch on the forward needle, then into the first stitch on the needle behind, and knit them together.

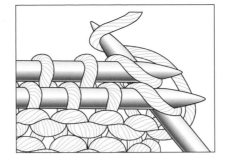

1 Insert the third needle into the first stitch on each needle, and knit them together. You have one stitch on the right-hand needle.

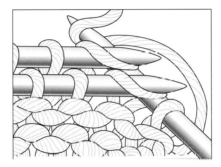

2 Insert the third needle into the next pair of stitches, and knit them together.

TIPS | DIY Network Crafts

Shaping Tip
For fully fashioned increases or decreases that present a neat, tailored appearance, work all increases and decreases one or two stitches in from the edge(s) of the knitting. This also makes seaming of pieces much easier.

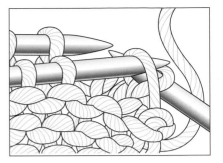

3 Pass the first stitch over the second.

◣ INCREASING STITCHES ◢

There are several ways to add a single stitch within your knitting. One of the simplest is to knit into the front loop and then into the back loop of the same stitch before slipping the stitch off the needle. You can use this technique for a decorative effect, while simultaneously shaping the knitting.

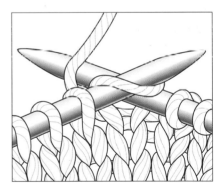

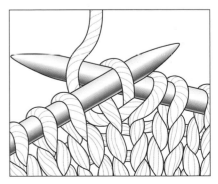

BASIC CROCHET STITCHES

Many knitting patterns are finished off with a crocheted edge. Crochet is not hard to learn and can make a beautiful trim for knitwear.

◣ MAKING A CHAIN ◢

To make a chain, first make a slip knot and place it on your hook. Wrap the yarn around the hook (yo), and pull it through the slip knot (loop). Repeat this step until you have the desired number of chains.

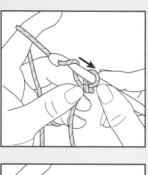

◣ SINGLE CROCHET ◢

Insert your hook into the space or stitch indicated. When working into a chain, insert hook into the second chain from the hook.

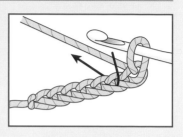

Yo and pull yarn back through the space or chain you went into. Yo hook again, and pull yarn through both loops on the hook. (1 loop remains on your hook.)

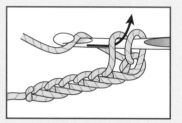

Repeat this process in each space or stitch across row. At end of row, ch 1 and turn the work to begin the next row.

◣ CROCHETING BACKWARDS ◢

Also known as "crab stitch" or "reverse single crochet," the backwards crochet stitch yields a textured, undulating decorative edge.

First work a row of regular single crochet. On the second row, ch 1, do not turn.

Instead, insert your hook into the stitch to the right of the beginning of the row (this will be the last stitch worked in the previous row). Yo and pull yarn through the stitch on the hook.

Yo again and pull through both loops on the hook, as for regular single crochet. Repeat this process, always working the next single crochet into the stitch to the right of the one just worked, until you reach the end of the row.

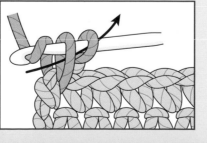

DECREASING STITCHES

Many methods exist to reduce the number of stitches on the needle.

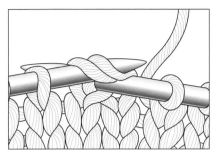

1 Two common ways are the k2tog and the ssk. The k2tog slants to the right and which means knitting two stitches together as one.

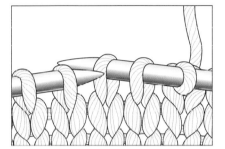

2 The ssk, which slants to the left. First you slip the first stitch as if to knit, and then slip the next stitch the same way.

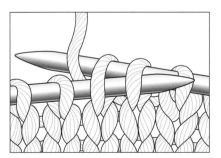

3 Next, insert the left-hand needle from left to right into the front of the two stitches just slipped, and knit the two stitches together through their back loops.

PICKING UP STITCHES

Knitting patterns often call for picking up stitches to add a finished edge to a knitted piece, and will instruct you to "pick up and knit" a certain number of stitches along an edge. Armhole or sleeve bands, front cardigan or jacket edgings, neckbands and afghan borders are typical examples. When you're picking up a large number of stitches, circular needles can be used to accommodate the width of the stitches on the needle. If you use circular needles in this way, treat them the same as straight needles, turning the needle after each row rather than joining the stitches in a circle. Beautifully finished bands are not difficult to achieve if you follow a few simple steps.

1 First, divide and mark the edges of the knitting where the stitches will be picked up into equal segments. Count the rows between the markers to ensure even spacing. (Safety pins work well as markers, because they won't fall out of the knitting.)

2 With the right side facing you, carefully separate the edge stitches so that you can see the small space (or hole) between the last two stitches at the end of each row. Push the needle through the hole to the back of the work, then place the yarn around the needle as if to knit, and draw a loop of yarn through with the needle. Continue along the edge in this way, picking up the stitches at a ratio of two stitches for every three rows. (In other words, you'll skip every third space.) If you're working along a garter stitch edge, pick up one stitch for every garter ridge. When you've picked up all the stitches, continue knitting the bands in the desired pattern stitch. Remember that the number of stitches you end up with is dependent on the number of rows in the edge you're picking up from. You may end up with a different number of rows than called for in your instructions if you've changed the length of the piece or if your knitting style or yarn choice changed the row gauge.

Bands worked in this way can make or break your garment's finished look, so it's important to make sure the number of stitches you've picked up fits your edge correctly. Try this method to check the fit. With a tapestry needle, thread a contrasting yarn color through your band stitches, and take the stitches carefully off the knitting needle. Adjust them evenly on this thread, so you can see how the band will look when bound off. If you have too many stitches, your edging will be wavy. If there are too few, your edging will pucker. Count the stitches and decide how many to add or remove. When you're satisfied, place the stitches back on the knitting needle and complete the bands.

◣ BLOCKING ◢

Blocking is the process of smoothing out the knitted pieces to the correct size and shape before you assemble them. The wet blocking method is simple, safe for all yarns, and always gives good results. To block a piece of knitting, first pin it out to the correct shape. Use blocking pins, which are made of stainless steel so they don't rust. Position the pins at regular intervals around the edges of the knitting, then check that the pieces are the correct size by comparing them to the schematic.

TIPS | DIY Network Crafts

Better fits

Don't skimp on edgings. If you are in any doubt about your bands, unravel the band and start again with more or less stitches. After all, if you hate the fit, you won't wear the garment, will you?

You'll need to work on a large, flat surface. Blocking boards designed for this purpose are available, or you can work on the floor with a towel under the knitting. Once your pieces are pinned out, spray them lightly with water and leave the knitting to dry. The effects of blocking are truly amazing: even stitches, great drape, and perfect shape!

◣ SEAMING ◢

With a little care, you can create beautiful seams, even if you don't ordinarily spend a lot of time with a sewing needle. In most cases, you'll work the seams with the same yarn you use for the knitting, but

SIZING GARMENTS

Length Chart

The Length Chart provides average lengths for children's, women's and men's garments.

	Waist Length	Hip Length	Tunic Length
Children	Actual body measurement	2"/5cm down from waist	6"/15cm down from waist
Women	Actual body measurement	6"/15cm down from waist	11"/28cm down from waist
Men	Men's length usually varies only 1–2"/ 2.5–5cm from the actual "back hip length" measurement.		

Fit Chart

Very-close fitting:	Actual chest/bust measurement or less
Close-fitting:	1–2"/2.5–5cm
Standard-fitting:	2–4"/5–10cm
Loose-fitting:	4–6"/10–15cm
Oversized:	6"/15cm or more

when the yarn is too textured to use easily, choose a smooth yarn in a matching color. Use a tapestry needle for seaming, and pin the seams together, if necessary, with knitter's pins. These are long and have a large head, so they don't disappear into the knitted fabric. Avoid working with a long length of yarn, as the friction may cause the yarn to break or fray.

◄ MATTRESS STITCH ►

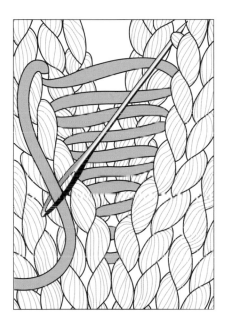

Mattress stitch is an excellent, all-purpose seaming stitch, resulting in an invisible seam. It's always worked with the right side of the work facing you, making it very easy to match stripes. To sew a seam in mattress stitch, first place the two pieces of knitting to be joined on a flat surface. Thread the needle and work upward one stitch in from the edge, passing the needle under the horizontal bar between the first and second

stitches on one side of the knitting, and then moving to the corresponding stitches on the other side. Pick up two bars and return to the first piece, going into the knitting at the same point you came out, and pick up two bars. Repeat these steps, working from side to side and pulling the seam closed as you go, taking care not to pull so tightly that you cause puckers. You want a flat, neat seam.

When seaming reverse stockinette pieces, use the same method, working into the purl "bumps" just inside each edge, and working into only one bump at a time throughout.

◄ MAKING BOBBLES ►

These are very useful embellishments on knitwear. They can be knitted in as the work is progressing, or added later. Brightly colored bobbles are a great way to enliven an otherwise plain sweater, while same-colored bobbles lend texture and elegance to knitted pieces. Many cabled, or Aran, sweaters, make generous

use of bobble stitches. The size of a bobble will vary, depending on the thickness of the yarn and the number of stitches you use.

1 Cast on one stitch, leaving a length of yarn to secure the bobble with, then k1, p1, k1, p1, k1 into the stitch before slipping it off the needle (5 sts).

2 Work 4 rows in St st on just these 5 stitches, turning the work as you normally would after each row.

3 Cut the yarn, thread it through a tapestry needle, and draw up tightly through the sts.

4 Fasten the bobble firmly into position.

METRIC/YARDAGE CONVERSIONS

To convert meters to yards, divide the metric measurement by .9144. To convert yards to meters, multiply the yardage amount by .9144.

1 cm = 0.394 inches

1 inch = 2.54 cm

1 yd = .9144 m

2

Wearable Knits

It doesn't matter whether you're hip, chic, funky, or fashion forward—knitting wearables with a creative edge is one style trend everyone can agree on. Why make a sweater when you can have a glamorous shrug, or mittens when you can create a beaded cuff or cabled gauntlets? Fabulous headgear from a camo ski hat to a Rasta cap, slippers knit in free-form, and a retro, furry, disco bag, are only some of the projects in this chapter that will get you knitting outside the box.

diy network

ROCK STAR BAG

"It's glorious!" If you recognize that lyric from the Breeders' debut album, you know this bag is the real deal. Trading guitar strings for yarn, rocker Kelley Deal created this gorgeous bag.

◣ **PROJECT SUMMARY** ◢

Even beginners will love making this bag. It's made by working stockinette stitch all the way. And the design, which looks like it's been knit, is embroidered with yarn and needle using an easy technique know as Swiss darning or duplicate stitch.

◣ Designed by **KELLEY DEAL** ◢

You Will Need

Approx 220 yds/201m of a worsted-weight 100% wool yarn in green heather (A)

Approx 100 yds/91m of same yarn in black (B)

Approx 20 yds/18m of same yarn in bright pink (C)

Needles in size 7 U.S. (4.5mm)

Needles in size 9 U.S. (5.5mm)

1½ yards (1.3m) of ¹⁴/₃₂" poly cord upholstery piping for Straps

Sewing needle with large eye

Large safety pin or diaper pin

Two-piece snap closure, approx ¾" (1.875cm) in diameter (optional)

Scissors

Tapestry needle

Extras

Gauge

4.25 sts and 6 rows = 1" (2.5cm) in St st, before felting, on larger needles

Finished Measurements

Height of Bag: 8" (20cm), not including Straps

Width of Bag: 11" (27.5cm)

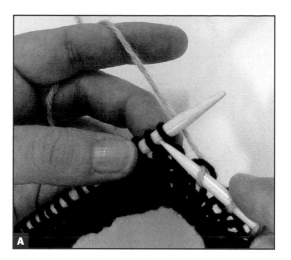

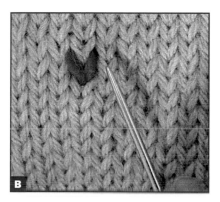

◢ MAKING THE BAG BODY ◣

1 With larger needles and B, CO 49 sts.
Rows 1-4: Work in St st with B.
Change to A (photo A).
Rows 5-145: Work in St st with A.
Change to B.
Rows 146-149: Work in St st with B.
With B, BO all sts.

2 Block Bag Body with steam iron on wool setting to flatten sts slightly and make them more even.

3 **Add Color Design** (photo B):
Count 33 rows down from top of Bag Body and locate center st in this row (this should be the 25th stitch in from either side edge.) Mark this as center st of Color Chart.

With tapestry needle and colors B and C, following Color Chart (see sidebar on page 33), work duplicate stitch embroidery onto Bag Body, taking care to place center st of Color Chart in same place as marked st on Body (photo C).

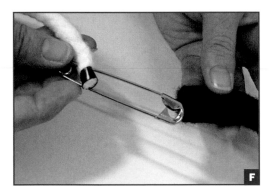

◣ FINISHING THE FELTED BAG ◤

4 Fold Bag in half and sew tog along side edges with tapestry needle and matching yarn, leaving top edge open (photo D).

5 **Make Straps:**
With smaller needles and B, CO 9 sts.
Work 120 rows in St st. BO all sts.
Repeat for second Strap. Fold Straps in half lengthwise and sew side edges tog to form a tube.

6 **Felting the Bag:** Set your washing machine to hot and use a heavy-duty cycle with low water. Add Bag and Straps to water after the agitation cycle begins. Repeat agitation cycle as necessary to achieve full felting and desired size, but do not let Bag and Straps go through the spin cycle. When the sts disappear and the Bag and Straps are slightly stiff, you have successfully felted them!

7 **Drying the Bag:**
At this point, squeeze Bag in a towel to remove excess water. Lay Bag flat on a table or other hard surface for drying, placing a book inside Bag to help shape it (photo E). Leave the book inside Bag and let dry overnight.

8 Use a large safety pin to help thread the piping through the tube of each Strap (photo F). Let Straps dry overnight, then trim excess piping and sew Strap ends closed.

9 **Assemble Bag:**
Pin Straps into place on inside of Bag (photo G). Using sewing needle and B, sew ends of Straps securely to inside of front and back of Bag.
Sew snap closures, if desired, to inside upper edges of Bag at center, between Strap ends (photo H).

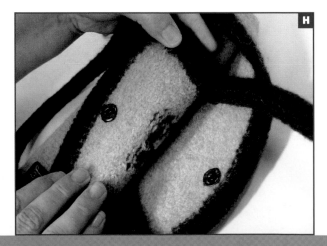

HOW TO WORK DUPLICATE STITCH ON KNITTED PIECES

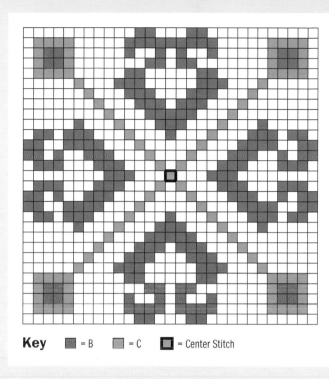

Key   ■ = B   ■ = C   ◻ = Center Stitch

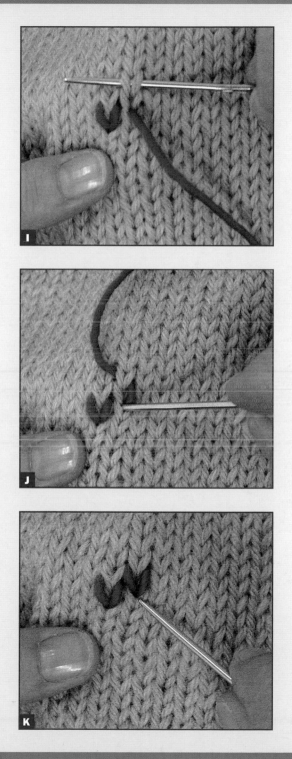

Thread a blunt needle with yarn color indicated by Chart. Bring the needle up in the center of the st, below the st to be worked, then take yarn under both halves of the "V" of the st to be worked (photo I). Bring yarn back down through the same space from which it came (photo J). Repeat this process for all remaining embroidered sts, following Chart carefully, and covering desired sts until Chart design is complete. Be sure not to pull too tightly on the embroidery yarn. The covering yarn should lie flat, and a bit above the covered st, to avoid puckering the knitting beneath it. When covering a block of adjacent sts, work diagonally rather than vertically if possible (photo K).

diy
network

RASTA HAT

You be jammin' man with this easy-going Rasta hat. If you're knitting to cover cascading dreads, the abundance of stitches in the pattern will accommodate them—you can even add more length to the hat if needed. If you're knitting for a sparser do, you can make the hat shorter. You can knit the brim, or not, and though shown in one color here, you can add stripes by using contrasting yarn.

◀ PROJECT SUMMARY ▶

You'll cast on and work in the round beginning with a knit-one, purl-one rib. The body of the hat is worked in stockinette stitch. You'll knit two eyelet rows, which you can make in contrasting colors for stripes. Simple decreases will complete the body. As a finishing touch, you'll pick up stitches for knitting the brim.

◀ Designed by **SHANNITA WILLIAMS** ▶

You Will Need

- Approx 275 yds/250m of a worsted-weight wool yarn
- Circular needle in size 6 U.S. (4mm), 16" (40cm) long
- Circular needle in size 8 U.S. (5mm), 16" (40cm) long
- 1 set dpns in size 8 U.S. (5mm)
- Tapestry needle
- Stitch marker
- Elastic thread in matching color (optional)

Extras

Gauge

4.5 sts = 1" (2.5cm) in St st

Finished Measurements

One size fits most adults.

MAKING THE HAT BODY

1 With smaller circular needle, CO 96 sts. Place marker and join in rounds, being careful not to twist sts around needle.

Rib Round: *K1, p1, rep from * around. Rep Rib Round until Hat meas approx 1½ inches from beg (photo A).

NOTE: If desired, carry elastic thread along with yarn throughout ribbing section, knitting each st with yarn and thread held tog. This makes the ribbing less likely to stretch with wear.

2 **Increase for Rasta Shape:** Change to larger circular needle. On next round, *k2, M1, rep from * around (photo B). (144 sts) Cont in St st, knitting all sts of every round, until Hat meas approx 4" from beg.

3 **Work Eyelet Round:** *Yo, k2tog, rep from * around (photo C).

Next 2 rounds: Knit.

Next round: Rep Eyelet Round.

NOTE: Eyelet Rounds are optional. You may substitute a different stitch pattern on these rows, omit

NOTES ON KNITTING IN THE ROUND

For an invisible join between rounds, choose from the following techniques:

Technique #1
Pass the first st on the RH needle over the last st on the LH needle and then begin knitting.

Technique #2
CO one extra st. Being careful not to twist sts, slip the first CO st to the RH needle and pass the last CO st over it, then move this st back to LH needle. Tug on the yarn end to close the circle. Then begin knitting.

Technique #3
CO required number of sts. Knit the first 2 rows flat, back and forth, and then join to knit in the round.

Technique #4
CO one extra st. Knit the last st and the first st together.

patterning altogether, or choose to knit these rows in a contrasting color for a subtle stripe effect.

Cont in St st until Hat meas approx 8-10 inches or desired length from CO row.

Next round: *K24, pm, rep from * to last 24 sts, k24. Six markers total should be on needle.

◣ SHAPING THE HAT TOP ◢

4 When working top shaping, switch to dpns when sts become too few to fit comfortably around the circular needle.

Shape Top:
Round 1: *SSK, k20, k2tog, rep from * around. (132 sts)
Rounds 2 and all even rounds: Knit.
Round 3: *SSK, k18, k2tog, rep from * around. (120 sts)
Round 5: *SSK, k16, k2tog, rep from * around. (108 sts)
Round 7: *SSK, k14, k2tog, rep from * around. (96 sts)
Round 9: *SSK, k12, k2tog, rep from * around. (84 sts)
Round 11: *SSK, k10, k2tog, rep from * around. (72 sts)
Round 13: *SSK, k8, k2tog, rep from * around. (60 sts)
Round 15: *SSK, k6, k2tog, rep from * around. (48 sts)
Round 17: *SSK, k4, k2tog, rep from * around. (36 sts)

Round 19: *SSK, k2, k2tog, rep from * around. (24 sts)

Round 21: *SSK, k2tog, rep from * around. (12 sts)

Round 22: Knit.

Cut 6-inch tail. Thread tail through rem 12 sts and pull to tighten. Weave in ends.

◀ MAKING THE BRIM ▶

NOTE: Brim includes instructions for three widths. Choose the width you prefer and follow that set of instructions.

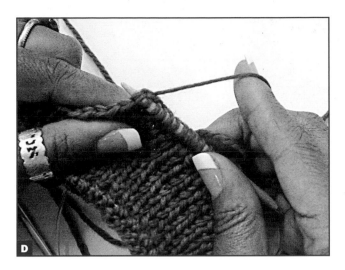

5 With dpn, pick up and knit 12 (14, 16) sts from center 12 (14, 16) CO sts of first round of Hat (photo D).

Row 1 (WS): Purl.

Row 2 (RS): K2, M1, pm, k8 (10, 12), pm, M1, k2 (photo E). Pick up next 2 sts knitwise from CO row.

Row 3: Purl across, then pick up and knit 2 sts purl-wise from CO row.

Row 4: K to marker, M1, slip marker, k 8 (10, 12) center sts, slip marker, M1, k to end. Pick up 2 sts knitwise from CO row.

Row 5: Purl across, then pick up and knit 2 sts purl-wise from CO row.

Rep Rows 4-5 until Brim meas approx 2" (5cm) from center of first Brim row, ending with a row 5.

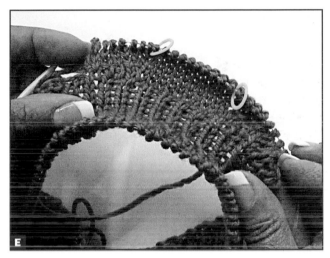

6 **Next row:** Purl for Turning Row.
Next row: BO first 2 sts, slipping first st before binding off rather than purling it. Purl across.

Next row: BO first 2 sts, slipping first st before binding off rather than knitting it. Knit to 2 sts before marker, SSK, slip marker, knit next 8 (10, 12) sts, slip marker, k2tog, knit to end (photo F).

Repeat last 2 rows until 12 (14, 16) sts rem.

BO rem 12 (14, 16) sts.

Turn under Brim along purl ridge of Turning Row and sew down to WS of Brim. Weave in all ends.

FIBONACCI SCARF AND WRISTLETS

It's no surprise that math and knitting go hand-in-hand. How else do you keep track of all those pattern stitches? Our designer took this connection a step further by introducing patterns based on the Fibonacci sequence—a series of numbers that relate to the Golden Ratio, which is found in nature and has long been used in art and design. Every number in the Fibonacci sequence is equal to the sum of the two numbers that precede it: 0, 1, 1, 2, 3, 5, 8, 13, 21, 34, 55... (we could go on, but it's time to have some fun!).

◀ PROJECT SUMMARY ▶

Get out your left-over yarn—any combination of textures and weights will do. There's no gauge restriction for the scarf, so mixing thick and thin yarns is just fine. You'll use a long-tail cast on, then work the garter stitch in one color. Change colors on any "Fibonacci" row, such as 1, 2, 5, 8, 13, etc. When you're finished, tie the two loose ends from each color change together, bring them to the front of the scarf, and let them dangle. You'll use lighter weight left-over yarn for the wristlets that are made using the garter stitch. You'll shape the thumb hole using a traditional bind-off and an easy three-needle bind-off.

◀ Designed by **ADINA KLEIN** ▶

You Will Need

Fibonacci Scarf

Scraps or leftovers of 9-15 different chunky to bulky-weight yarns in varying textures, in chosen color family

Needles in size 11 U.S. (8mm) or size 13 U.S. (9mm), depending on how thick your yarns are. Choose the higher size needle if most of your yarns are bulky-weight.

Fibonacci Wristlets

Scraps or leftovers of 8-10 heavy worsted to chunky-weight yarns in varying textures, in same color family as yarns for Scarf

Needles in size 10 U.S. (6mm)

Extra needle in size 10 U.S. (6mm)

Both Projects

Crochet hook, size K/10.5 U.S. (6.5mm)

Tapestry needle

Extras

Gauges

Fibonacci Scarf: Gauge can vary and is not crucial for this pattern

Fibonacci Wristlets: 4 sts = 1" (2.5cm) in St st

Finished Measurements

Fibonacci Scarf: Depending on yarns used, Scarf will measure from 3" to 5" (7.5cm to 12.5cm) wide and 55" (137.5cm) long

Fibonacci Wristlets: Approx 8½" (21.25cm) long and 8" (20cm) in circumference

◀ MAKING THE FIBONACCI SCARF ▶

1 With larger ndls and desired yarn, CO 13 sts loosely. Knit two rows (one ridge made on RS).

**[Continue in G st (knit every row) until there are 1, 2, 3, 5, 8 or 13 ridges on the RS (any number in the Fibonacci sequence will do; the choice is entirely up to you!)

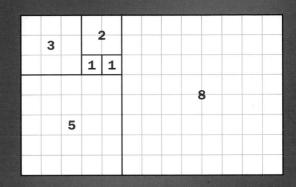

WHERE DOES THE 'FIBONACCI' COME FROM?

For many milennia, mathematicians have been fascinated by the expression of the "golden ratio"— φ

The Fibonacci Series

$$0 + 1 = 1$$
$$1 + 1 = 2$$
$$1 + 2 = 3$$
$$2 + 3 = 5$$
$$3 + 5 = 8$$
$$5 + 8 = 13$$
$$8 + 13 = 21 \ldots$$

(Greek letter *phi*)—In naturally occuring forms such as shells, sunflowers, and other spiraling things. Fibonacci was a 13th-century mathematician who discovered that a particular sequence of numbers yielded similar "golden ratio" properties. He started with "0" and placed a "1" next to it, added those two numbers together to get "1" again, then added the last two numbers ("1" and "1") together to get "2," then added the last two numbers together ("1" and "2") to get "3," and so on. The Fibonacci sequence, as it has since been called, looks like this: (0, 1, 1, 2, 3, 5, 8, 13, 21...) For many centuries since this discovery, architects and designers (even poets!) have been taking advantage of the "golden ratio" inherent in the Fibonacci sequence to create works of great beauty. And now, you can too! Just let each number of the sequence represent a number of rows or ridges in each color or yarn stripe. Try it, but be warned—Fibonacci knitting can be addictive!

Cut yarn, leaving a long tail, and join in next desired yarn. On next row, weave tails in slightly as you knit by bringing the working yarn under and over the yarn tail, alternately, for several inches. Leave tails hanging this way, in the middle of the work, until later (photo A, above).

Rep from **, changing yarns at desired Fibonacci number of ridges throughout, until Scarf meas approx 55" (137.5cm) from beg, ending with a RS row.

BO all sts loosely. The last ridge made by binding off completes your last Fibonacci ridge.

TIPS | DIY Network Crafts

Spit Splicing

To seamlessly blend your new yarn into the old in the middle of a project, try spit splicing the ends together. You can try this trick with any animal fiber. First, moisten the ends of both pieces of yarn, then overlap the ends and rub them together between your palms. It may take a while, but eventually you'll get a smooth, durable join.

2 Finishing the Scarf:
To fasten off the yarn tails that were left hanging while knitting, take two tails and tie them tog with an overhand knot. Next, using the crochet hook, pull one of the tails through to the other side of Scarf, leaving one tail hanging on either side. Repeat for all tails. If desired, trim all tails to a shorter and even length.

◢ MAKING THE FIBONACCI WRISTLETS ◣

Casting on with the Provisional (Crochet) Method:

1 With crochet hook and smooth waste yarn, make a slip knot around hook and ch 40. Cut waste yarn and tie a knot at end of last chain st. Set crochet hook aside.

2 With smaller knitting needle and desired working yarn, working into the "bumps" along the underside of the crocheted chain, pick up and knit one st into each bump, leaving all picked-up sts on needle. Continue in this way until 34 sts are on your needle (photo A, facing page, top left). (Extra chains are okay; they will be removed later.)

3 With smaller needles, work in Fibonacci ridge pattern as for Scarf, knitting every row and working only 1, 2, or 3 ridges for each stripe. Weave yarn tails toward the center of the Wristlet as before. Continue until Wristlet meas approx 8" (20cm) from beg, or until Wristlet fits comfortably around your wrist, ending with a RS row. Leave sts on needle; do not bind off.

4 Finishing the Wristlet:
Return to lower CO edge of Wristlet and cut away the slip knot at one end of the crochet chain. Holding one knitting needle near work, pull slowly on the yarn tail released by cutting the knot. The chain will begin to "unzip" and reveal loose sts of main yarn in your CO row (photo B). Place these sts carefully onto knitting needle as you unzip the chain. When all sts have been placed on the needle, discard waste yarn.

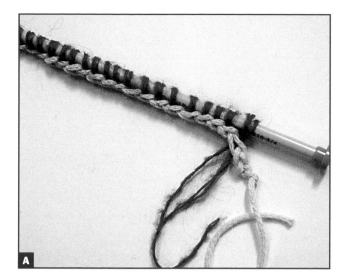

5 **3-Needle Bindoff:**
Make sure that both knitting needles (one at CO edge and one at upper edge) are facing with their points in the same direction. (If needles are facing in opposite directions, simply transfer the CO sts to the extra needle by slipping them one by one to the extra needle.)

Fold Wristlet in half so that needles are parallel on top, with WS of Wristlet facing you. With the third knitting needle, go into first st on front needle and then into first st on back needle, and knit these 2 sts tog (photo C). * Work the next sts from each needle tog in the same way, then pass first st on working needle over the second st on working needle (one stitch bound off (photo D).

Continue from * across until all sts have been bound off. Cut yarn and bring tail through last st. Pull tightly to close.

Using crochet hook, knot and separate yarn ends along Wristlet as for Scarf.

Make a second Wristlet—either identical to the first, or in a slightly different color and yarn sequence, as desired.

WILD & CRAZY HATS

If your style is way more improvise than compromise, let the world know it. After all, you are what you wear. Both hats start with a simple knit structure before breaking into their own wild and crazy design frenzy. Fun to knit and to wear, they're sure to get the funky vibe going wherever you go.

◣ **PROJECT SUMMARY** ◢

You almost think you're knitting a regular hat—circular needles, stockinette stitch, decreases to shape—then you get to the cylinder that just seems to grow right out of your needles. The hardest part of making this hat is deciding how many more cylinders you can add to it. And, if you think the other hat looks like an inside-out bowl of spaghetti, you're right. The trick to making it is to create holes as you knit for stringing the I-cord. The more holes you make, the more loops of spaghetti you can have on your hat—of course, you can never have too many. Go for it!

◣ Designed by **JOHN BRINEGAR** ◢

You Will Need

Spaghetti Bowl Hat, Right:

Approx 216 yds/198m of a chunky-weight alpaca yarn

Circular needle in size 10 U.S. (6mm), 16" (40cm) long

1 set of dpns in size 10 U.S. (6mm)

Claudia's Cylinder Hat, Left:

Approx 206 yds/188m of a chunky-weight multicolor yarn

Circular needle in size 8 U.S. (5mm), 16" (40cm) long

Circular needle in size 10 U.S. (6mm), 16" (40cm) long

1 set dpns in size 8 U.S. (5mm)

1 set dpns in size 10 U.S. (6mm)

Wool roving or polyfill stuffing

Both Hats:

Tapestry needle

Stitch marker

Extras

Gauges

Spaghetti Bowl Hat: 4 sts = 1" (2.5cm) in St st

Claudia's Cylinder Hat: 3.5 sts = 1" (2.5cm) in St st

Finished Measurements

To fit average size child or small adult.

---

holes all over hat by working (yo, k2tog) at random throughout (photo B). For effect, the hat should have at least 30-40 holes (yos).

3 NOTE: When working top shaping, switch to dpns when sts become too few to fit comfortably around the circular ndl.

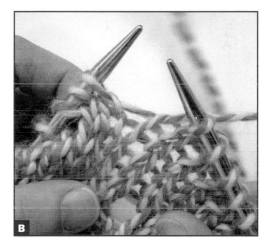

◄ MAKING THE SPAGHETTI BOWL HAT ►

1 With larger circular ndl, CO 72 sts. Place marker and join in rounds, being careful not to twist sts around ndl.

Rib Round: *K2, p2, rep from * around. Rep Rib Round 4 times more (photo A).

2 Beg knitting all sts of every round until Hat meas approx 6" (15cm) from beg, incorporating

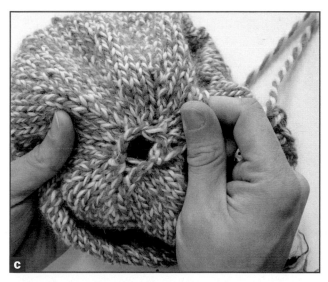

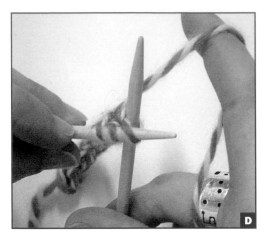

Shape Top:

Round 1: *K2tog, k6, rep from * around. (63 sts)

Rounds 2, 4, 6, 8, 10: Knit.

Round 3: *K2tog, k5, rep from * around. (54 sts)

Round 5: *K2tog, k4, rep from * around. (45 sts)

Round 7: *K2tog, k3, rep from * around. (36 sts)

Round 9: *K2 tog, k2, rep from * around. (27 sts)

Round 11: *K2tog, k1, rep from * around. (18 sts)

Round 12: *K2tog, rep from * around. (9 sts)

BO all sts, leaving a small hole in top of Hat (photo C, preceding page).

◤ FINISHING THE SPAGHETTI BOWL HAT ◢

4 Using one dpn, CO 3 sts and work an I-cord at least 6 feet (1.82m) long (photo D). BO sts and weave in ends of cord.

5 Thread the I-cord through the holes in your Hat, weaving in and out, leaving lengths of I-cord hanging on the ouside and pulling I-cord flat against the inside of Hat as you go (photo E). Secure I-cord ends inside Hat (photo F).

6 Put your spaghetti bowl atop your head and wear!

◤ MAKING CLAUDIA'S CYLINDER HAT ◢

1 With larger circular ndl, CO 72 sts. Place marker and join in rounds, being careful not to twist sts around ndl.

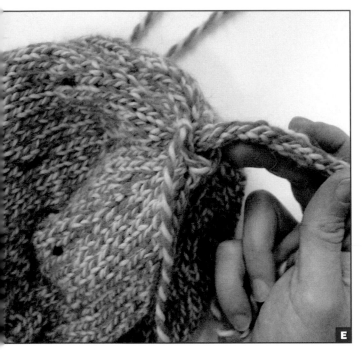

Knit all sts of every round until Hat meas approx 6" (15cm) from beg (photo A).

2 NOTE: When working top shaping, switch to dpns when sts become too few to fit comfortably around the circular ndl (photo B).

Shape Top:

Round 1: *K2tog, k6, rep from * around. (63 sts)

Rounds 2, 4, 6, 8, 10: Knit.

Round 3: *K2tog, k5, rep from * around. (54 sts)

Round 5: *K2tog, k4, rep from * around. (45 sts)

Round 7: *K2tog, k3, rep from * around. (36 sts)

Round 9: *K2 tog, k2, rep from * around. (27 sts)

Round 11: *K2tog, k1, rep from * around. (18 sts)

3 Change to smaller dpns and continue knitting rounds on the rem 18 sts until the resulting "cylinder" meas approx 9". BO all sts (photo C).

◣ FINISHING CLAUDIA'S CYLINDER HAT ◢

4 Stuff wool roving or polyfill inside cylinder just made from the inside of Hat until it takes on a uniform shape (photo D). Bend the cylinder over and attach to side of Hat by sewing it down onto the surface.

5 **Additional Cylinders:** With dpns, CO 18 sts. Knit in rounds until cylinder meas desired length. BO. Make as many cylinders as you would like. Attach as for center cylinder by sewing to surface of Hat, positioning cylinders as desired (photo E). The more, the funkier! Weave in all ends and wear!

FREEFORMIN' FEET

These funky diva slippers will put you in a knitting frenzy. This is one project where you can free your stitches and spirit at the same time. Your needles will move quickly from stitch to stitch as you learn the basics of freeform style. All this and embellishments too? Get out the beads, sequins, and charms, it's time to cut yourself footloose and fancy free.

You Will Need

1 pair of mesh Chinese slippers

Scraps or small amounts of 7 different medium- to worsted-weight novelty yarns

1 set dpns in size 4 U.S. (3.5mm)

1 set dpns in size 5 U.S. (3.75mm)

Medium-size crochet hook for edgings

Embroidery scissors or other small scissors

Assorted beads or charms (you can also use the sequins or beads from the slippers once you've removed them)

Sewing needle

Tapestry needle

Extras

Gauge
Gauge is not crucial to this freeform pattern.

Finished Measurements
To fit around medium-size slippers. The sizing is easily adjustable by working extra motifs, or adding/subtracting a few rows as desired to fit your slipper.

◢ PROJECT SUMMARY ◣

These slippers are made with a technique known as freeform knitting. Small pieces of highly textured fabric, which inventors Sylvia Cosh and James Walters named "scrumbles," are made in various stitch and yarn combinations, then joined together to create one-of-a-kind items, from wearables to wall hangings. No rules, no patterns, nothing but fun!

◢ Designed by **MYRA WOOD** ◣

Rep Rows 3-4 until leaf is as wide as you like. It's up to you! Cont even in St st (or g st) for several rows until you'd like to start decreasing.

Next Row: Sl 1, k1, psso, work in desired st patt to last 2 sts, k2 (or p2) tog as desired.

Rep last row, dec one st at each end of each row as before, until 3 sts rem.

Next Row: Sl 1, k2 tog, psso. Cut yarn, leaving a long tail for sewing, and thread tail through last st.

2 **Knit slip st around edge** (photo B): With contrast yarn and smaller dpn, pick up and knit 1 st at corner edge of Leaf. Pick up and k another st and slip the first picked-up st over the second. Pick up next st. Continue to pass previous st over each

◢ MAKING THE FIRST SCRUMBLE ◣

1 **Leaves (make 2 in different colors):** With smaller dpns, CO 3 sts (photo A).

Row 1: K3.

Row 2: P3.

Row 3: Knit into front and back of first st (inc made), k to last st, knit into front and back of last st (inc made). (5 sts)

Row 4: Purl into front and back of first st (inc made), p to last st, purl into front and back of last st (inc made). (7 sts)

new picked-up st until entire Leaf is edged with slip st. Cut yarn, leaving a long tail, and thread tail through 1 rem st.

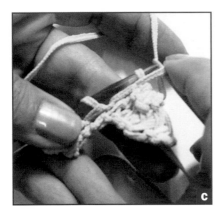

3 **Half-Round** (photo C): Using larger dpns and a new color of yarn, CO 13 sts. Knit back and forth in rows for 3 rows.

Row 4: Knit 1 and place this knitted st back onto LH needle. Beginning with the second st on LH needle, pass each of the last 12 sts, one at a time, over the first knitted st and off the needle (photo D). Use a crochet hook to do this if preferred.

Turn work and pick up 1 st from beginning of row, just before the point where you knit the first st. 2 sts are now on the needle. Pass the first st over the picked-up st. Cut yarn, leaving a long tail, and thread tail through rem st.

4 Place the two Leaves next to each other with the Half Round between them and use the yarn tails to stitch them tog with a whipstitch on the WS of work, making one piece (photo E). Cut sewing yarn, leaving a short length for tucking between the slipper fabrics later.

5 **Rice Stitch Triangle:** RS facing, with a new yarn color and larger dpns, pick up and knit an odd number of sts along one straight side of one Leaf.

Purl one row.

Row 2: *P1, k1 tbl, p1, rep from * to end.

Row 3: Knit.

Row 4: Sl 1, k1, psso, k to last 2 sts, k2tog.

Row 5: Work as for Row 2.

Rep Rows 4-5 until there are 3 sts on needle.

Next Row: Sl 1, k2tog, psso. Cut and thread tail through last st.

6 Turn work so WS is facing you. With crochet hook, join an eyelash yarn with a slip st to one corner of Triangle. Ch1 and work a row of sc halfway around the entire Scrumble piece as follows: Start on one side, work up over the rounded area, and work halfway down the other side.

◀ MAKING THE SECOND SCRUMBLE ▶

7 **Full Round:** Using a new yarn and larger dpns, CO 21 sts. Work 3 rows in St st.

Next Row: Work as for Row 4 of Step 3, slipping all 20 sts over the first knitted st. Turn work and pick up 1 st from beginning of row, just before the point where you knit the first st. 2 sts are now on the needle. Pass the first st over the picked-up st. Cut yarn, leaving a long tail, and thread tail through rem st. With RS facing and crochet hook, join a contrast yarn with a slip st to any point on the Full Round (photo F). Ch1 and work 1 round of sc around entire edge. (You may need 2 sc in some sts in order to ease around the edge and keep work flat.) Cut yarn, leaving a long tail. Thread this tail through the last st on hook. Using tail, stitch this round to one edge of the First Scrumble, measuring against the slipper to make sure it sits comfortably in the top of the slipper.

8 **Fill in the V** (photo G): RS facing, with larger dpns and a new yarn, pick up and knit 3 sts in the bottom (point) of the V between Scrumbles.

Row 1: K1, p1, k1, pick up 1 st from the left side of the V as it faces you (photo H).

Row 2: K1, p1, k1, p1, pick up 1 st from the left side of the V as it faces you.

Continue in this manner, knitting all k sts and purling all p sts, picking up one st from side of V at end of each row, until V area is filled in. BO all sts.

◀ FINISHING THE SLIPPERS ▶

9 Make Bobbles (MB) into indicated sts as follows: (k1, yo, k1, yo, k1) into st, then turn work and purl the 5 sts just made, then turn work again and knit these 5 sts, then turn work and (k1, sl 1, k2tog, psso, k1), then turn work and (sl 1, k2tog, psso). One Bobble made.

10 **Bobble edging:** RS facing, with smaller dpns and a new yarn, pick up and k 9 sts along any straight edge of combined Scrumbles piece.

Row 1 (WS): Purl.

Row 2 (RS): MB into first st, k1, *MB into next st, k1, rep from * to last st, MB into last st. (5 Bobbles)

Row 3: Knit. BO all sts.

Knit Bits:
TOP FIVE TIPS FOR STARTING A KNITTING GROUP

Number Five
Find a location. Make sure you choose a public place. Newcomers are less likely to come to a private home. It's important that the location is well lit, smoke free, and easily accessible.

Number Four
Start an Internet posting group. Starting an Internet group is the fastest, easiest way to create community amongst your group.

Number Three
Communicate. Make flyers and post them in public spaces. Ask your local yarn storeowner to give them out to customers.

Number Two
Stay consistent. Once you pick a day and time for your regular meetings, stick with it. People are more likely to come to meetings that they know they can count on.

Number One
Keep it fresh. To keep people excited about the group, plan knitting-oriented field trips and parties. One popular type of party is the knitting potluck. Invite friends to bring their favorite yarns, or yarns they've always wanted to try. By the end of the evening, everyone can have a simple scarf made of lots of swatches.

11 **Making the Rosettes:**
With 2 larger dpns and desired yarn, CO 15 sts.
Row 1: (Knit into front and back of st) in each st across. (30 sts)
Row 2: (Knit into front and back of st) in each st across. (60 sts)
BO, leaving a long tail for sewing.
Roll flower into shape.
With yarn tail, sew bottom of Rosette tog to hold flower shape (photo I).

12 With embroidery scissors, cut off and remove all beads, sequins, etc. from slippers (photo J). Put these aside.
Using tapestry needle and desired yarn color, whip-stitch assembled freeform slipper top around mesh portion of slipper, easing as necessary to fill in and fit the entire space. Tuck all yarn ends and seam ends between slipper mesh and knitted slipper top.

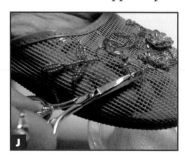

Using thread and sewing needle, reattach beads and sequins as desired to embellish knitted freeform slipper tops (photo K).

LACE SAMPLER SHRUG

The greatest thing about knitting a sampler is that you get to learn new stitches—all on one piece. With this project, you'll not only increase your lace stitch vocabulary, you'll have a great shrug to show for it. If you want to take it even further, you can throw a combination of different chunky yarns in the mix to make a truly one-of-a-kind signature piece.

You Will Need

Approx 975 yds/891m of a chunky-weight yarn

1 pair needles in size 11 U.S. (8mm)

Crochet hook, size K/10.5 (6.5mm)

Tapestry needle

Extras

Gauge

2.5 sts and 3 rows = 1" (2.5cm) in St st

Finished Measurements

Width of rectangle (before sewing): 14" (35cm)

Length from cuff to cuff (before sewing): 55" (137cm)

Notes

All sts will be very loose.

Width of rectangle may vary until piece is seamed and blocked to an even width.

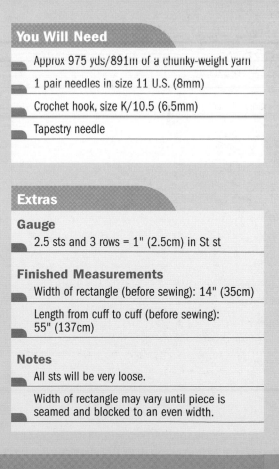

◄ PROJECT SUMMARY ►

There's no complicated shaping in this project because the shrug is made from a large knit rectangle that you fold in half. This makes working (and learning) new stitches a breeze since you won't have any extra increases or decreases to slow you down. Some of the stitches included in the pattern are simple eyelet stitch, staggered seeded eyelet, filet-ribbed lace, double dropped stitch, and monster bobble. To keep the pattern stitches separate, you'll knit a few rows of garter stitch in between. After you seam the arms, you'll finish the edges with single crochet.

◄ Designed by MYRA WOOD ►

◄ MAKING THE SHRUG ►

1 CO 34 sts loosely.
Rows 1-4: Work in G st (knit every row) for four rows.
Simple Eyelet Patt (photo A):
Row 5: K1, *yo, k2tog, rep from * to last st, k1.
Row 6: Knit.
Rows 7-10: Rep Rows 5-6, twice.
Rows 11-14: Knit.

2 **Staggered Seed Eyelet Patt:**
Row 15: K1, *yo, k2tog, rep from * across to last st, k1.
Row 16: *K1, p1, rep from * across.
Row 17: K1, *p2tog, yo, rep from * across to last st, k1.
Row 18: *P1, k1, rep from * across.
Rows 19-30: Rep Rows 15-18, 3 times more.
Rows 31-39: Knit.

3 **Double Dropped St Patt:**
Row 40: *(K1, yo) twice, rep from * to last st, k1.
Row 41: Knit across, dropping all yos.
Pull downward on piece to stretch dropped sts evenly (photo B).
Rows 42-49: Knit.

4 **Filet Ribbed Lace Patt:**
Row 50: K1, *yo, sl 1, k2tog, psso, yo, k1, rep from * to last st, k1.
Row 51: Knit.
Row 52: Work as for Row 50.
Row 53: K1, purl across to last st, k1.
Rows 54-61: Rep Rows 50-53, 2 times more.
Rows 62-65: Knit.
Rows 66-70: Work in St st, but knit first and last st of all WS rows.
Rows 71-73: Knit.

5 **Single Dropped St Patt:**
Row 74: *K1, yo, rep from * across to last st, k1.
Row 75: Knit all knit sts and drop all yos.
Rows 76-77: Knit.

6 **Alternating Eyelet Patt:**
Row 78: K1, *yo, k2tog, rep from * to last st, k1.
Row 79: Knit.
Row 80: Work as for Row 78.
Row 81: Knit.
Rows 82-89: Rep Rows 78-81, 2 more times.
Rows 90-97: Knit.

7 **Monster Bobble Patt:**
Row 98: Knit.
Row 99: Purl.
Rows 100-101: Knit.
Row 102: *(K1, yo twice), rep from * to last st, k1. (98 sts)
Row 103: Knit the knit sts and the first wrap of each yo, dropping each second yo wrap. (66 sts)
Row 104: K1, *p2tog, rep from * to last st, k1. (34 sts)
Rows 105-108: Knit.

8 **Ribbed Eyelet Patt:**
Row 109: K1, *yo, k2tog, rep from * to last st, k1.
Row 110: *K2, p2, rep from * to last 2 sts, k2.
Row 111: *P2, k2, rep from * to last 2 sts, p2.
Row 112: K1, *yo, k2tog, rep from * to last st, k1.
Rows 113-114: Rep Rows 110-111.
Rows 115-119: Knit.

9 **Checkerboard Patt:**
Row 120: *K4, p3, rep from * across to last 2 sts, p2.
Row 121: K2, *p4, k3, rep from * across to last 4 sts, p4.
Row 122: *P4, k3, rep from * across to last 2 sts, k2.
Row 123: P2, *k4, p3, rep from * across to last 4 sts, k4.

10 **Windowpane Lace Patt:**
Row 124: K2, *yo, k2tog, rep from * across to last 2 sts, k2.
Row 125: *K3, p2, rep from * across to last 4 sts, k3, p1.
Rows 126-129: Rep Rows 124-125, 2 times more.
Rows 130-132: Knit.

11 **Simple Eyelet Patt:**
Row 133: K1, *yo, k2tog, rep from * across to last st, k1.
Row 134: Knit.
Rows 135-136: Rep Rows 133-134.
Rows 137-138: Knit.
BO loosely.

FINISHING THE SHRUG

12 Fold rectangle in half from side to side lengthwise. (Rectangle will be just as long but only half as wide now.)
Measure 17" down from each end for sleeve cuffs. Pin these 17" sections tog, leaving center of rectangle open.
Sew sleeve seams, using mattress stitch.
With crochet hook, join yarn with a slip st to one underarm seam. Ch1 and work a row of sc evenly spaced around entire opening. Join with a slip st to first sc. Ch1 and work a second row of sc around, working 1 sc into each sc of previous round. Join with a slip st to first sc. Fasten off.
Work 1 round of sc around each sleeve cuff in the same manner. Fasten off. Weave in ends.

TIPS | DIY Network Crafts

Russian Join
There's a great technique called the Russian Join for connecting ends when a new ball of yarn is incorporated into a project. To employ this technique, fold over the two ends of yarn and thread a needle onto one end. Sew the end of the yarn back onto itself. Repeat with the end of the other strand of yarn and trim off the loose ends.

CAMO HAT

Wearing camouflage usually means you want to blend into the background. But if extreme is more your style on the slopes or city streets—this bright ski hat is for you. Made by using variegated yarn, you get a fabulous multi-colored effect without changing strands. The crocheted and braided trim add even more flair. And that big orange pom-pom? You've got to love it.

◼ PROJECT SUMMARY ◼

Using straight needles, you'll make each ear flap separately. The body of the hat is knit in stockinette stitch using circular needles. For a seamless transition between flaps and cap, you'll pick up the flap stitches as you cast on stitches for the body. Easy decreasing shapes the hat, and simple single crochet trims it. The braided ties extend the fun, while the large, luscious pom-pom tops it all off.

◼ Designed by **THE SOUZA FAMILY** ◼

You Will Need

Approx 140 yds/128m of a bulky-weight wool yarn in camouflage variegated (MC)

Small amount (less than 10 yds/9m) of same yarn in bright orange (CC)

Circular needle in size 10 U.S. (6.5mm), 16" long (40cm)

1 set dpns in size 10 U.S. (6.5mm)

Tapestry needle

Stitch marker

Extras

Gauge

3 sts = 1" (2.5cm) in St st

Finished Measurements

Sized for Small (Large). Finished Hat circumference is approx 20"/50cm (22"/55cm). Instructions are given for size Small, with instructions for size Large in parentheses. Make sure to follow instructions for chosen size throughout.

MAKING THE EAR FLAPS AND HAT BODY

1 **Ear Flaps (make 2):**
With dpns or circular needle and MC, CO 7 sts.
Row 1 (WS): Purl. Turn to work in rows.
Row 2 (RS): Inc in first st by knit into front and back of st, knit to last st, inc as before (photo A). (9 sts)
Row 3: Purl.
Row 4: Knit, inc into first and last st as for Row 2. (11 sts)
Row 5: Purl.
Row 6: Knit, inc into first and last st as for Row 2. (13 sts)
Work even on 13 sts until Ear Flap meas approx 3" (7.5cm) from beg, ending with a WS row (photo B). Cut yarn and place these 13 sts on a holder.
Work another Ear Flap to match, ending with a WS row. Place sts of second Ear Flap on circular needle.

2 **Begin Body of Hat:**
With circular needle and MC, knit across 13 sts of second Ear Flap, turn work and CO 20 (24) sts onto LH needle for back of Hat.
Turn work. Holding first Ear Flap with RS facing you, knit across 13 sts. Turn work and CO 14 (16) sts onto LH needle for forehead side of Hat. You should have 60 (66) sts total (photo C). Place marker and join into a circle, being careful not to twist CO sts around needle.
Work even in St st (knit every round) until Hat meas approx 6"/15cm (7"/17.5cm) from beg, not including Ear Flaps (photo D).

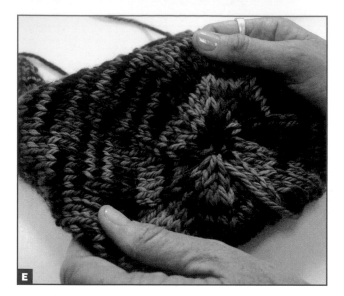

◄ SHAPING THE HAT TOP ►

3 NOTE: When working top shaping, switch to dpns when sts become too few to fit comfortably around the circular needle.

Shape Top:

Round 1: *K4, k2tog, rep from * around: 50 (55) sts.

Rounds 2 and all even rounds: Knit.

Round 3: *K3, k2tog, rep from * around: 40 (44) sts.

Round 5: *K2, k2tog, rep from * around: 30 (33) sts.

Round 7: *K1, k2tog, rep from * around: 20 (22) sts.

Round 9: *k2tog, rep from * around: 10 (11) sts.

Cut 6-inch (15cm) tail. Thread tail through rem sts and pull to tighten. Weave in ends (photo E).

◄ FINISHING THE HAT ►

4 **Crochet edging:** RS facing, with crochet hook and CC, join yarn with a slip st at lower edge of back of Hat. Ch1, work 1 sc in same space as joining slip st. Work 1 round of sc evenly spaced around entire Hat, working 3 SC into lower point of each Ear Flap (photo F).

5 **Braid Trim:** Cut 6 lengths of MC yarn, 24" (60cm) long, and 6 lengths of CC yarn, 24" (60cm) long. Take 3 lengths of each color (6 strands total) and lay them side-by-side into a bundle, alternating colors. Repeat this process to make a second bundle.

Holding ends of yarn strands tog, pull one bundle of strands through Hat at lower point of one Ear Flap until half of the length of bundle is on either side of Ear Flap. (Using a crochet hook to pull the strands through is helpful.) Fold bundle so that all ends meet at the bottom and press bundle as flat as possible with fingers. You should have 12 strands hanging down below the Ear Flap point after folding.

Divide strands into 3 groups of 4 strands each, taking care to include 2 strands of each color in each group, and braid strands tog until braid is desired length (photo G).

Wrap a separate strand of yarn tightly around lower end of braid, knot and secure ends.

Repeat this process with second bundle of yarn strands on opposite Ear Flap.

If desired, make a large pompon with CC and attach to top of Hat.

◢ PROJECT SUMMARY ◣

You'll find there's no end to glamour when you combine I-cord with beads. By sewing the ends of the I-cord together, you create the knit circles that become the basic motif for each piece. For the earrings, you'll string beads on a head pin as you insert them into the circles; for the necklace, you'll string a series of circles and beads together using the same cord you use for knitting the I-cord; and, you'll make the cute double ring by embroidering two circles together with beads in between. It's just that easy—so, no excuses!

◢ Designed by **KELLY WILSON** ◣

SHIMMERY JEWELRY

Knit jewelry—how fabulous is that? Now you can forget those old excuses about not having jewelry to match an outfit. This complete ensemble is built around an I-cord circle that you string with beads. Once you make one piece, you'll find it's easy—and irresistible—to make the rest. Even if you've never worked with beads before, this project is definitely quick. What are you wearing tonight?

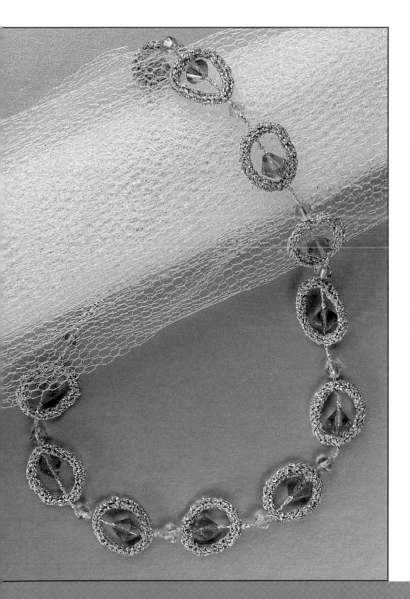

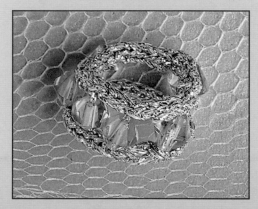

You Will Need

Crystal Ring
- 3 blue-colored bicone beads, 6mm
- 3 lime-colored bicone beads, 6mm

Crystal Earrings
- 4 blue-colored bicone beads, 6mm
- 2 lime-colored bicone beads, 8mm
- 2 silver head pins, 2" (5cm)
- 2 silver earring wires
- Round-nose pliers
- Wire cutters
- Jeweler's glue (optional)

Crystal Necklace
- 13 blue-colored bicone beads, 8mm
- 14 lime-colored bicone beads, 6mm
- Silver jewelry clasp
- 2 silver crimp beads with knot covers
- Chain-nose pliers
- Jeweler's glue (optional)

All Projects:
- Needles in size 0 U.S. (2mm)
- Embroidery needle
- Beading needle (optional)
- 50 yds. (45m) very fine, synthetic metallic yarn

A

Extras

Gauge for All Projects
Knitted I-cord should measure ⅛" (0.3125cm) wide when laid flat.

Finished Measurements
Crystal Ring: Adjustable to actual size of finger

Crystal Earrings: 2" (5cm) long, not including earring wire

Crystal Necklace: 14" (35cm) long

◢ MAKING THE CRYSTAL RING ◣

1 CO 3 sts.
Work I-cord as described in the sidebar on the opposite page until I-cord measures same length as circumference of desired ring finger.
BO, leaving a long tail for sewing.
Using embroidery ndl, sew CO and BO ends tog to create a circle.
Weave in ends.

2 **Finishing the Crystal Ring** (photo A):
Using the attached yarn tail, insert embroidery ndl through the side of one of the Rings. Slide on a blue bead.
Insert ndl into the side of the second ring to secure bead (bead will be between the two Rings).
Move the ndl through the I-cord tube and bring ndl out where the next bead will be placed.
Slide on a lime bead.
Insert ndl into the side of the opposite ring to secure bead (bead will be between the two Rings).
Continue in this way, spacing beads evenly between Rings all the way around, and securing beads between the two Rings.
Weave in ends.

◢ MAKING THE CRYSTAL EARRINGS ◣

1 Make 2 Rings as for Crystal Ring, making each I-cord 2" (5cm) long.
Slide a blue bead onto a head pin.
Insert head pin through one end of one Ring.
Slide on a lime bead.
Insert the head pin into the opposite side of the Ring.
Slide on a blue bead.

Apply a small amount of jeweler's glue (if desired) to both ends (inside the holes) of the lime bead to hold it in place.
Let the head pin dry on a flat surface.

2 Cut head pin with wire cutters, leaving approx ½" (1.25cm) exposed.
Bend the exposed wire to make a 90 degree angle (photo B).

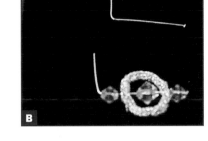

HOW TO MAKE I-CORD

Cast on the number of stitches indicated onto one needle (see photo above). *Knit one row. Do not turn work, but slide sts across to right end of needle. Bring yarn tightly across back of work from end of knitted row. Repeat from * until I-cord tube reaches desired length.

Using round-nose jewelry pliers, curve the exposed end of the head pin into a loop.
Place the earring wire loop through the head pin loop. Close the head pin loop.
Repeat for second Crystal Earring, using remaining Ring.

◀ MAKING THE CRYSTAL NECKLACE ▶

1 Make 13 Rings as for Crystal Ring, making each I-cord 2" (5cm) long.

2 **Stringing the Necklace:**
Cut a 24" (60cm) length of yarn and thread into embroidery or beading ndl.
Slide a lime bead onto thread.
Push ndl through one side of one Ring and tie a knot. If desired, jeweler's glue may be used in place of knots.
Slide a blue bead onto ndl and tie a knot.
Insert ndl through opposite side of Ring.
Slide a lime bead onto ndl.

3 Repeat Step 2 12 more times, adding Rings to necklace with beads placed as for first Ring.

4 **Finishing the Crystal Necklace:**
Insert one end of the 24" (60cm) length of yarn (now strung with beads and Rings) through crimp bead with knot cover. Double knot and cut excess yarn. Place a small amount of glue on knot, if desired. Add clasp to the hook on the crimp bead (photo C). Use jewelry pliers to close.

DISCO SET

If you're looking for a little disco glam and don't know where to start, check out this cute ensemble with a snugalicious purse. This knit halter top and metallic shrug will turn heads under the disco ball. Made with two kinds of glittery, fuzzy yarn, the bag feels as good as it looks. Large, gold-ring handles add a touch of funky-retro bling.

◀ PROJECT SUMMARY ▶

This bag is so easy, you could make it in a few hours to wear tonight. Knit on straight needles using the garter stitch, the bag has easy-shape tops that fold over to accommodate the handles. You'll knit two separate pieces, attach the handles, seam it all together, and rock on out the door. Dy-no-mite!

◀ Designed by **BRETT BARA** ▶

You Will Need

Silver and Gold Shrug

Approx 110 (110, 165) yds/100 (100, 150)m of a worsted-weight synthetic metallic fur-type yarn in gold (A)

Approx 110 (110, 165) yds/100 (100, 150)m of same yarn in silver (B)

Needles in size 13 U.S. (9mm)

Halter

Approx 345 yds/315m of a worsted-weight acrylic/cupro metallic tape yarn in dark purple (C)

Circular needle in size 8 U.S. (5mm), 24" (60cm) long

Crochet hook, size D/3 U.S. (3.25mm)

Disco Purse

Approx 230 yds/210m of same yarn as Halter in same dark purple (C)

Approx 78 yds/70m of a bulky-weight eyelash yarn in dark purple with bright blue and purple slubs (D)

Needles in size 3 U.S. (3.25mm)

Waste yarn, worsted-weight, in black

2 bangle handles

All Projects

Tapestry needle

Stitch marker

Extras

Gauges

Shrug: 3 sts and 4 rows = 1" (2.5cm) in g st (knit every row) with size 13 (9mm) ndls and one strand each of A and B held together

Halter: 5 sts and 7 rows = 1" (2.5cm) in St st with size 8 (5mm) circular needle

Disco Purse: 4 sts = 1" in g st (knit every row) with size 3 (3.25mm) needles

Finished Measurements

NOTE: Shrug and halter patterns are written for smallest size, with changes for larger sizes in parentheses. When only one number is given, it pertains to all sizes. Take care to follow instructions for your chosen size.

Shrug: Width 18½ (21, 23)" [46.25 (52.5, 57.5)cm]; Length 7 (8, 9)" [17.5 (20, 22.5)cm]

Halter: Width 27 (28, 29)" [67.5 (70, 72.5)cm], stretches to fit 34 (36, 38)" [85 (90, 95)cm] bust; Length 15½ (16, 16½)" [38.75 (40, 41.25)cm]

Disco Purse: 6½" (16.25cm) wide and 8½" (21.25cm) long

A

◣ MAKING THE SILVER AND GOLD SHRUG ◢

1 With size 13 (9mm) ndls, holding one strand of A and B tog, loosely CO 42 (48, 54) sts (photo A).

Work in g st (knit every row) for 1½ (1½, 2)" [3.75 (3.75, 5)cm]

2 **Dec Row 1 (RS):** K2 tog, knit to end of row. (41, 47, 53 sts rem)

Dec Row 2 (WS): Knit to last 2 sts, k2tog. (40, 46, 52 sts rem)

Rep (Dec Rows 1-2) until 22 (24, 28) sts rem.

Inc Row 1 (RS): Knit into front and back of first st, knit to end of row. (23, 25, 29 sts)

Inc Row 2 (WS): Knit to last st, knit into front and back of last st. (24, 26, 30 sts)

Rep (Inc Rows 1-2) until there are 42 (48, 54) sts.

Work even in g st for 1½ (1½, 2)" [3.75 (3.75, 5)cm] more.

BO loosely.

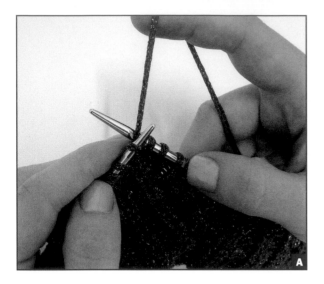

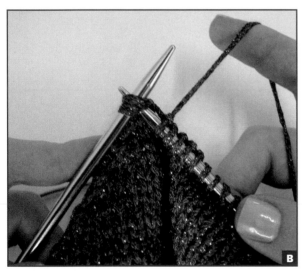

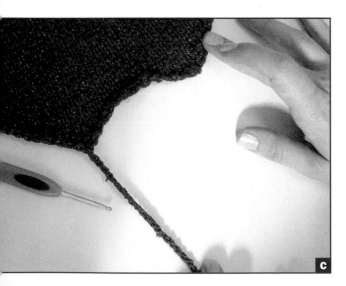

3 **Finishing the Shrug:**
Fold Shrug in half lengthwise and sew 1½ (1½, 2)" [3.75 (3.75, 5)cm] underarm seams where ends of g st rows meet.
Weave in ends.

◢ MAKING THE HALTER ◣

1 With circular needle and C, CO 136 (140, 144) sts. Place marker and join, being careful not to twist sts around needle.
Rib Round: *K1, p1, rep from * around (photo A).
Rep Rib Round, 53 (55, 57) times more.

2 Working in St st, BO 15 sts, knit across rem 121 (125, 129) sts, turn and begin working back and forth in rows.
Row 1 (RS): *P2tog, p to last 2 sts, p2tog. (119, 123, 127 sts rem)
Row 2 (RS): *K2tog, knit to last 2 sts, k2tog. (117, 121, 125 sts rem)
Rep (Rows 1-2) until 25 sts rem, ending with a RS row.

3 **Shape Neck:**
Next Row (WS): P2tog, p8, drop working yarn, join a second ball of yarn and BO 5 sts, purl across until 2 sts rem, p2tog. (9 sts rem each side)
Working both sides at same time with separate balls of yarn, continue as follows (photo B, bottom left):
Row 1 (RS): K2tog, k5, k2tog. (7 sts rem each side)
Row 2: P2tog, p3, p2tog. (5 sts)
Row 3: K2tog, k1, k2tog. (3 sts)
Row 4: P3tog. BO last st.

4 **Finishing the Halter** (photo C):
RS facing, with crochet hook and C, beg at top point of right neck, join yarn with a slip st to Halter body. Ch1, work 1 sc in each row end, in each bound-off st at back, and in each row end to top point of left neck. Fasten off.
Ties:
With crochet hook and C, ch 90, work 1 sc in top point of left neck, work sc evenly across front neck to top point of right neck, ch 90. Fasten off.
Weave in all ends.

◣ MAKING THE DISCO PURSE ◥

1 Purse Body (Make 2):
With smallest needles, and holding one strand each of C and D tog, CO 24 sts (photo A).
Work in g st (knit every row) until Purse meas approx 7" (17.5cm) from beg.

2 Shape top of Purse:
Cont in g st, knitting first 2 sts tog at beg of every row, until 12 sts rem.
Work even on these 12 sts for 2" (5cm) more.
BO loosely. Make a second Purse Body the same.

3 Finishing the Purse:
To attach handles, fold the narrow "neck" at top of one Purse Body over a bangle handle and stitch in place using black waste yarn (photo B). (Note: Photo shows contrast yarn for illustration purposes only.)
Repeat for second Purse Body and second bangle handle.
Stack Purse Bodies with attached handles one on top of the other, RS facing out. Line up bottoms, sides, and handles carefully, then stitch Purse Bodies tog along sides and lower edge with black waste yarn (photo C).

A

B

TIPS | DIY Network Crafts

Polishing old needles

What do you get when you combine uncooked rice with your needles? You get a great new way to polish up old wooden needles. Just pour some uncooked rice into a tall container, then dip your needles in the cup several times. This makes old, sticky needles smooth and gives them a new-car shine.

C

PERFECT COMBO SHRUG

Just like beans and rice, shoes and socks, and wash and dry, knit and crochet is one of those classic combos. So, let's get ready to mix it up. The easy knit-and-purl repeat of the pattern gives the shrug its wonderful texture, while the frilly crochet edging adds a perfect complement for a finishing touch. Wear this piece with jeans and a tee, or over a cute little dress.

◀ PROJECT SUMMARY ▶

This is a great project for learning how to introduce crochet into your knitting. Using straight needles, you'll knit the back of the shrug first. Next you'll knit each side separately, shaping them with a series of increases. After you finish knitting the arms, you'll sew the side and shoulder seams before sewing the sleeves onto the body. Using a crochet hook and a contrasting color of yarn, you'll make the slightly scalloped edging by combining single crochet with chaining.

◀ Designed by **CANDI JENSEN** ▶

You Will Need

Approx 820 yds/744m of a heavy worsted weight cotton yarn in main color (MC)

Approx 205 yds/186m of a heavy worsted weight cotton yarn in contrast color (CC)

1 pair needles in size 9 U.S. (5.5mm)

Crochet hook, size G/6 (4mm)

1 button, approx 1" (2.5cm)

Tapestry needle

Extras

Gauge

4.5 sts and 6 rows = 1" (2.5cm) in rib patt st

Finished Measurements

Chest: 32 (36, 40)" [80 (90, 100)cm], Length: 12 (13, 14)" [30 (32.5, 35)cm]

Rib Pattern Stitch

Row 1: Knit

Row 2: *K1, p1, rep from *, ending with a k1.

Rep Rows 1-2 for rib patt st.

MAKING THE BACK

1 With MC, CO 73 (81, 91) sts.

2 Work in rib patt st until Back meas 12 (13, 14)" [30 (32.5, 35)cm] from beg. BO in patt.

MAKING THE LEFT FRONT

3 With MC, CO 11 (14, 17) sts. Work in rib patt st, increasing 1 st at the right side edge on every row 24 (25, 26) times. (35, 39, 43 sts)

4 Work even for 1" (2.5cm) more, then dec 1 st at the right side edge on every other row 16 (18, 22) times. (19, 21, 21 sts). Work even until same length as Back to shoulder.

MAKING THE RIGHT FRONT

5 For Right Front, work as for Left Front, working all incs and decs at left side edge of piece (photo A).

MAKING THE SLEEVES

6 With MC, CO 51 (53, 55) sts. Work in rib patt st, increasing 1 st at each side edge every 4th row 12 (13, 14) times (photo B). (75, 79, 83 sts) Work even in patt until Sleeve meas approx 9 (9, 10)" [22.5 (22.5, 25)cm] from beg. BO in patt.

A

B

FINISHING THE SHRUG

7 Sew shoulder and side seams. Sew sleeves onto body.

8 **Crochet edge:** With RS facing, CC and crochet hook, join yarn with a slip st to the left shoulder seam. Ch1 and work 1 round of sc around entire body of shrug by working (1 sc for every st and 1 sc for every 2 rows) around. Join with a slip st to first sc.
Next round: *Sc, ch 3, sk 2 sc, sc in next sc, rep from * around (photo C). Join with a slip st to first sc of round.
Next round: *Sc in next st, work (2 hdc, sc) in next ch-3 space, rep from * around. Join with a slip st to first sc of round. Fasten off (photo D).

9 Sew button in place. Weave in all ends.

Knit Bits:
POLYMER CLAY NEEDLE HEADS

Is fighting with your fellow knitsters over whose needles are whose a familiar scene to you? It doesn't have to be — just learn to personalize your needle heads! First, get some polymer clay in various colors. Roll the clay into a ball and press the end of your needle into the clay. Since the clay shrinks slightly when baked, stretch the opening slightly by rotating the needle. Remove the needle, then bake the clay according to the manufacturer's instructions. Once cooled, place a drop of adhesive on the end of the needle and a drop inside the opening of clay. Place the clay back on the end of the needle and let the adhesive set. You'll never have to argue with your friends again. (About needles, anyway!)

Designed by **AMY FINLAY**

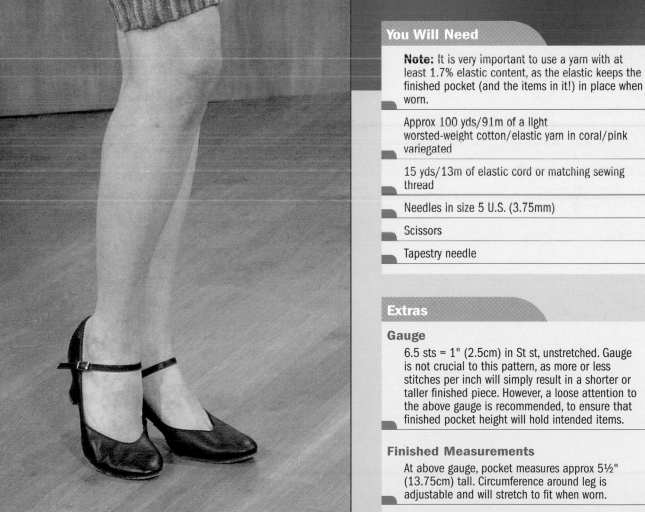

GARTER POCKET

Keep the stash, ditch the trash. If you're into traveling light, knit a cozy thigh garter to hold your must-haves—money, lipstick, cell—as you gad about town hands-free. Let the garter peek seductively from a skirt's side slit. Or, if you want to keep it secret, cut an opening in the pocket of your pants or skirt for hidden access.

You Will Need

Note: It is very important to use a yarn with at least 1.7% elastic content, as the elastic keeps the finished pocket (and the items in it!) in place when worn.

Approx 100 yds/91m of a light worsted-weight cotton/elastic yarn in coral/pink variegated

15 yds/13m of elastic cord or matching sewing thread

Needles in size 5 U.S. (3.75mm)

Scissors

Tapestry needle

Extras

Gauge

6.5 sts = 1" (2.5cm) in St st, unstretched. Gauge is not crucial to this pattern, as more or less stitches per inch will simply result in a shorter or taller finished piece. However, a loose attention to the above gauge is recommended, to ensure that finished pocket height will hold intended items.

Finished Measurements

At above gauge, pocket measures approx 5½" (13.75cm) tall. Circumference around leg is adjustable and will stretch to fit when worn.

A

B

C

PROJECT SUMMARY

For a snug but comfortable fit, you'll knit the garter on straight needles using elastic yarn. (Look for some great tips from our designer for keeping the garter in place.) The first few stitches of each row create the lacy top of the garter, otherwise, it's—what else?—garter stitch all the way. Once you've knit the diameter you need to go around your thigh, you'll bind off stitches in preparation for knitting the pocket flap. When you're finished, you'll seam the flap to the garter, stitching separate pockets to size for your essentials. So, who needs a purse?

MAKING THE GARTER POCKET

1 **Pocket Body:**
CO 36 sts, leaving a long tail before casting on for use later in finishing.

Row 1 (RS): K1, *k2tog, yo, yo, k2tog, rep from * once, knit to end of row.

Rows 2, 4 (WS): Knit across, except over double yos: for double yos, knit into first yo and purl into second yo.

Row 3: K3, *k2tog, yo, yo, k2tog), rep from * once, knit to end of row.

TIPS | DIY Network Crafts

Knitting with Elastic Yarn

When knitting with elastic yarn, tension can be tricky. Try not to stretch the yarn fully when knitting with it. Instead, stretch it only slightly so that it is not completely taut. Experiment with the yarn in a small swatch to determine the best way to achieve consistent tension. Often, wrapping the yarn one extra time around your finger, or weaving the yarn through fingers, helps to control the uniformity of the knitted piece.

Repeat Rows 1-4 until Pocket Body is long enough to stretch around your leg when fully stretched, ending with a Row 4 (photo A).

2 **Overlapping Pocket Flap:**
BO 16 sts at beg of the next row.
Work in g st (knit every row) over rem 20 sts until Flap section is about ⅓ as long as the Pocket Body (photo B). BO all rem sts.

◀ FINISHING THE GARTER POCKET ▶

3 Using tail from CO row, sew the CO row of the Pocket Body to the last row of Pocket Body where you bound off 16 sts, leaving remaining edges of Pocket Flap unsewn. Sew loosely to allow for stretching when worn.

4 Turn Pocket Flap down so that it curls around bottom half of Pocket Body and stitch in place along lower edge. Sew loosely as before, to allow for stretching (photo C).
Sew BO edge of Pocket Flap to Pocket Body. You now have one large Pocket attached to Pocket Body.

5 Try on Pocket and place sample items in Pocket Flap. Mark their size and desired position within Pocket Flap, then sew vertical rows of stitches along marked points to top of Flap, sewing through both Flap and Pocket Body (photo D). This creates compartments for your items.

KEEPING THE POCKET IN PLACE ON THE LEG

Here are some tips for keeping the Pocket in position. One very clever idea is to sew the Pocket to a favorite pair of leggings or nylons. Make sure to do this while wearing both items to ensure a good fit later.

Another option is to run strands of elastic thread in parallel rings along the inside of the Pocket, catching the g st ridges (photo E). Join each ring of stitching by pulling the elastic thread to desired tension and knotting the ends of the thread. Ideally, you'll want about 12 of these sewn rings of elastic, with one at the top edge, another at the bottom edge, and the rest spaced evenly between. Use matching elastic, if possible, or dye the elastic to match your yarn before sewing.

diy
network

RECTANGLE PONCHO

This just might be the rectangle revolution you've been waiting for. If you've mastered the art of knitting by making scarves for everyone you know—including your ex—it's time to step outside the box. This fabulous poncho will help you re-invent the rectangle. Depending on the yarn you use, it can look like a glam fur from the 1940s or become a sultry wrap for dressing up your basic black.

◣ PROJECT SUMMARY ◢

Poncho is knit as a long rectangle and then folded, leaving an opening for the head. The piece is knit in St st and then every few sts are dropped down to the CO row to allow for a looser fit and to create a more open look. This Poncho can be turned in any direction depending on where you prefer to have the extra fabric.

◣ Designed by **FAYLA REISS** ◢

You Will Need

Approx 720 yds/656m of a worsted-weight synthetic blend woven yarn with flags and short chenille slubs in blue/green variegated (A)

Approx 400 yds/366m of a polyester/viscose worsted-weight yarn in shiny metallic teal/black variegated (B)

Approx 50 yds/46m of a chunky-weight silk ribbon tape yarn in green/dark green variegated (C)

Approx 100 yds/92m of a chunky-weight silk ribbon tape yarn in greyish blue/green variegated (D)

Needles in size 9 U.S. (5.5mm)

Crochet hook, size G/6 U.S. (4mm)

Tapestry needle

Extras

Gauge

Gauge is not critical as long as the indicated weight yarns are used. The beauty of rectangle-based patterns is that you can be off by an inch or two—or more—without affecting the integrity of the design. Experiment with fun textures and colors as you like!

◀ MAKING THE RECTANGLE PONCHO ▶

1 With size 9 (5.5mm) needle and holding one strand of A and B tog, CO 83 sts.

Row 1 (RS): *K4, k2tog, yo, rep from * across row, ending with k5.

Row 2 (WS): Purl across.

Rep Rows 1-2 until Poncho meas approx 56" (140cm) from beg, ending with a RS row.

Next Row: *K5, drop 1 st off the LH needle, rep from * across, ending with k5 (photo A).

2 **Finishing the Poncho:**
Pull all dropped sts back to the very beginning, which should be a yo from the first row.
Stretch piece to open up the knitting (photo B).
Block rectangle with light steam and a damp cloth.

3 RS facing, with size G/6 (4mm) hook and C or D, join yarn with a slip st to one corner of Poncho. Ch1 and work 1 row of sc evenly

spaced around 3 sides of Poncho, leaving rem side unworked. Fasten off.

Fold Poncho in half so that two edged sides are touching and rem edged side is at the bottom. Turn folded Poncho so that unworked side edge is at your left. Beg at lower left corner, sew unworked side edge tog from bottom up, leaving 12" (30cm) unworked at top for head opening.

RS facing, with size G/6 (4mm) hook and C or D, join yarn with a slip st to any spot on neck opening. Ch1 and work 1 round of sc evenly spaced around entire neck opening. Fasten off.

Weave in ends.

SOCK IT TO ME

Treat your feet—socks are on the way.
Follow the instructions from cuff to toe, and
your cold tootsies will thank you.

■ PROJECT SUMMARY ■

If you've put off knitting socks because you just
couldn't face all those double-pointed needles
or you thought that turning the heel would be
too hard, be brave and knit on. Once you get the
hang of it, you'll find that socks are quick to knit
and make perfect portable projects.

◢ Designed by KAREN BAUMER ◣

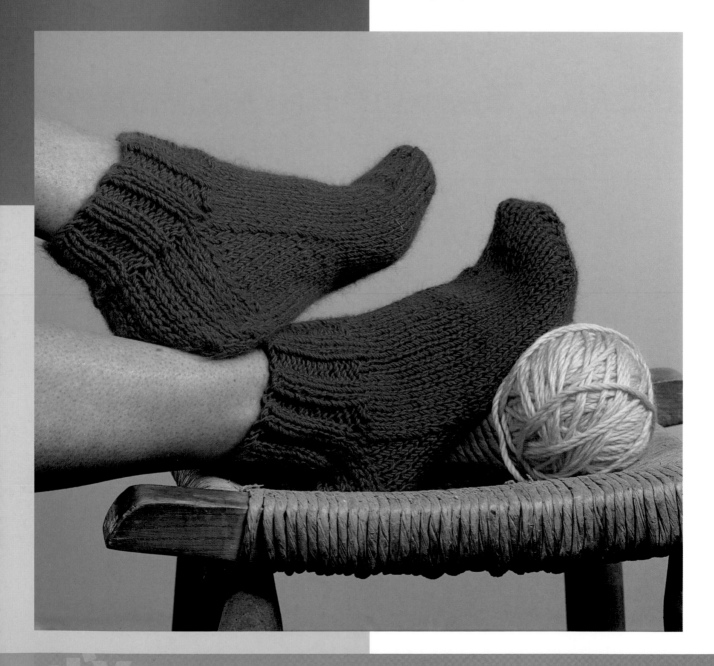

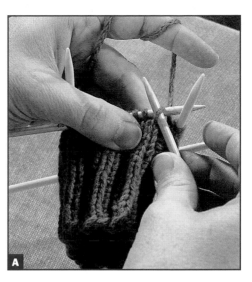

You Will Need

Approx 263 yds (240m) of a worsted-weight angora/wool/nylon blend yarn

1 set of 5 double-pointed needles in size 7 U.S. (4.5 mm)

Tapestry needle

Stitch marker

Extras

Gauge

5 sts and 7.5 rows = 1" (2.5cm) in St st worked in the round

Finished Measurements

To fit average width foot and lower leg. May be adjusted as desired.

◣ STARTING THE CUFF ◣

1 Loosely CO 40 sts and divide evenly among 4 of the dpn's. Join into a circle, being careful not to twist stitches around the needles. Place marker to mark beg of round.

Round 1: *(K2, p2), rep from * around.

Rep Round 1 until Cuff meas approx 2.5" (6.25cm), ending with a completed round (photo A).

◣ MAKING THE HEEL FLAP ◣

2 **Row 1 (RS):** *Sl 1, k1, rep from * across next 20 sts with a single needle and turn, leaving rem 20 sts unworked on rem needles.

Row 2 (WS): Sl 1, p to end.

Rep Rows 1-2 on these 20 sts, back and forth on 2 dpns as with regular straight ndls, until Heel Flap meas approx 2.75" (6.8cm) long, ending with a RS row (photo B).

3 **Turning the Heel** (photo C).
Row 1 (WS): P11, p2tog, p1, turn.

Row 2 (RS): Sl 1, k3, SSK, k1, turn.

Row 3: Sl 1, p4, p2tog, p1, turn.

Row 4: Sl 1, k5, SSK, k1, turn.

Row 5: Sl 1, p6, p2tog, p1, turn.

Row 6: Sl 1, k7, SSK, k1, turn.

Cont in this manner, adding one st worked before the dec in each row, until all of the sts have been worked, ending with a RS row. 12 sts rem on working needle.

▰ MAKING THE GUSSET ▰

4 Divide your heel sts in half, leaving the last 6 sts just worked on current needle and sliding first 6 onto an empty needle. With RS of work facing you, using current needle, pick up and k 12 sts (one st per slipped st) along left side edge of Heel Flap (photo D). With empty needle, cont knitting across next 10 "resting" sts. With empty needle, k across rem 10 "resting" sts. With empty needle, pick up and k 12 sts along right side of Heel Flap, then k across 6 sts from beg of row. Sts should be divided as follows: 18 sts on first and fourth ndls, and 10 sts on second and third ndls. Place marker and join to work in rounds.

▰ SHAPING THE GUSSET ▰

5 Cont in St st as follows:
Round 1: K6, k tbl of rem sts on first needle; k across sts on second and third ndls; k tbl across sts of fourth needle until 6 sts rem, k6.
Round 2: K until 3 sts rem on first needle, k2tog, k1; k across sts on second and third ndls; k1, SSK across first 3 sts on fourth ndl; knit to end of round.
Round 3: Knit.
Rep Rounds 2-3 until 10 sts rem on all four ndls (photo E). (40 sts)

▰ MAKING THE FOOT ▰

6 Cont in St st until the foot of the sock is about 7" (17.5cm) long measured from the back of the heel, or about 2" (5cm) shorter than desired finished length (photo F).

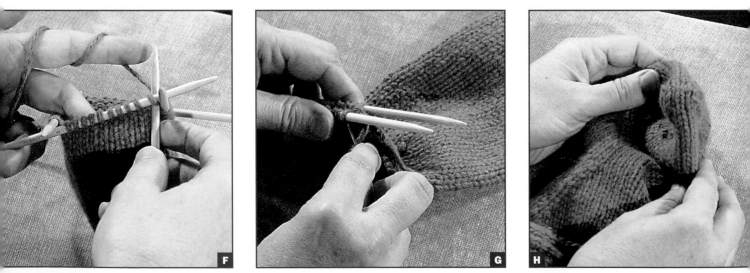

◖ SHAPING THE TOE ◗

7 **Round 1:** K to last 3 sts on first needle, K2tog, k1; k1, SSK, k to end of second needle; k to last 3 sts on third ndl, K2tog, k1; k1, SSK, knit to end of round.

Round 2: Knit.

Rep Rounds 1-2 until 12 sts rem. K across first needle, leaving rem sts unworked. Rearrange sts on two ndls, so that top and bottom foot sts are parallel and yarn is coming from needle holding bottom foot sts (photo G). Cut yarn, leaving a 10-12" (25-30cm) tail.

◖ FINISHING THE SOCK ◗

8 Graft the toe tog using kitchener st. Weave in any rem yarn ends (photo H).

GRAFTING

Grafting is a way to join two groups of knit stitches without sewing them together. When you graft, you add a new row of knitting between the existing stitches, using a tapestry needle and yarn. It's not only a magical way of creating stitches from thin air—it's also incredibly useful for seamless joins of all kinds.

Grafting is typically used to join sock toes, shoulder seams, or the underarm stitches of yoked sweaters. At first glance, grafting may seem intimidating, but it isn't difficult, and takes only a little practice. Once you master grafting, you'll wonder what you did without it!

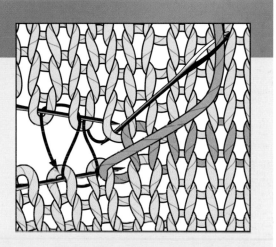

1 Arrange stitches on two needles so that wrong sides of fabric are facing each other and the RS of work faces you.

2 Thread a tapestry needle with matching yarn, allowing approx 1" (2.5cm) of yarn per stitch to be grafted.

3 Note: Work from right to left across sts to be grafted.

Step 1-F (front half of first step): On the front needle, bring yarn through first st as if to purl. Leave this st on the needle.

Step 1-B (back half of first step): On the back needle, bring yarn through first st as if to knit. Leave this st on the needle.

Step 2-F (front half of second step): On the front needle, bring yarn through first st as if to knit, and slip this st off the needle. Then bring yarn through next st as if to purl, and leave this st on the needle.

Step 2-B (back half of second step): On the back needle, bring yarn through first st as if to purl, and slip this st off the needle. Then bring yarn through next st as if to knit, and leave this st on the needle.

4 **Repeat Steps 2-F and 2-B** until all sts have been grafted. When you are done, use the tapestry needle to tug gently at the thread you've used, adjusting the tension of your grafted row of knitting to match the tension of the rest of the knitting.

diy
network

COOL LIDS

After sweating geometry, did you ever think triangles could be so cool? The knit helmet, inspired by a geodesic dome, is made by sewing equilateral triangles together. And if you're wondering how many you need to make for a custom fit, an easy formula will help you figure it out. The From-the-Top hat is knit from the top down. Instead of decreasing to shape, you increase, which gives you lots of opportunities to improvise your own design from start to finish.

◾ **PROJECT SUMMARY** ◾

For the Sundown Hat, you'll figure the width of the base of the triangles once you know the diameter of the head you're knitting for—and from there it's pure geometry. If this makes you want to stop reading, don't. Our designer practically gives you the answer. You might even find working the math fun. The From-the-Top Hat is knit in the round using double-pointed needles. The pattern, as knit, makes a close-fitting stocking hat, but you can knit it longer or fuller, or make it even more hip with pom-poms, tassels, or a custom cuff.

◾ Designed by **LISA ANNE AUERBACH** ◾

You Will Need

Sundown Hat, Left

Approx 250 yds/228m total of scraps or different colors of a worsted-weight wool yarn

Needles in size 7 U.S. (4.5mm) or circular needle in same size, any length

Crochet hook, size H/8 U.S. (5mm) for edging

From-the-Top Hat, Right

Approx 250 yds/228m total of scraps of different colors of a worsted-weight wool yarn

Circular needle in size 6 U.S. (4mm), 16" (40cm) long

Circular needle in size 5 U.S. (mm), 16 (40cm) long

1 set dpns in size 6 U.S. (4mm)

Both Hats:

Tapestry needle

Stitch marker

Extras

Gauges

Sundown Hat: 4.5 sts = 1" (2.5cm) in St st

From-the-Top Hat: 5.5 sts = 1" (2.5cm) in St st with larger needles

Finished Measurements

To fit average size adult. If gauge is exact, each Hat will meas approx 21" (52.5cm) in circumference after assembly.

◀ MAKING THE SUNDOWN HAT ▶

1 **Basic Triangle** (make 18 for Hat without ear flaps or 26 for Hat with ear flaps):

CO 16 sts.

Row 1 (RS): Knit.

Row 2 (WS): P2tog, purl to last 2 sts, p2tog. (2 sts decreased)

Rep (Rows 1-2) until 1 st rem. Cut yarn, leaving a long tail for sewing, and draw tail through last st to secure (photo A).

2 **Construct the Hat:**
**Hold one Triangle so that one flat edge runs along bottom and point is at top. Take a second Triangle and place it in same manner next to first Triangle (photo B). Lower inner points of Triangles should be all that are touching. Take a third Triangle and position it upside down between first 2 Triangles, so that point of third Triangle faces down and third Triangle fills the space between the first 2 Triangles. Using attached yarn tails in matching colors, sew these three Triangles tog in this position. Rep from ** twice more, so that you have 3 groups of 3 Triangles each. Position a new Triangle upside down between each 3-Triangle group and stitch in place to join all 3 groups tog into a ring.

3 For top of Hat, take one Triangle and position it point-up. Take a second Triangle and position it point-up next to first Triangle. Sew these two Triangles tog along their inner edges, beg at point where their lower inner corners touch. This will cause both upper points to meet at the top and will cause the lower edge to form an angle.

*Take another Triangle and position it point-up next to first 2 joined Triangles. Join tog along inner edges as before. Rep from * until 6 Triangles have been joined, then form into a cone with upper points on top and sew inner edges of end Triangles tog.

Sew top cone of Hat to lower ring of Hat, matching flat edges of each Triangle around (photo C).

4 **Ear Flaps** (make 2, optional):
For each Ear Flap, make one 3-Triangle group as for lower ring of Hat. Take a fourth Triangle and position it point-up along flat edge of the middle (upside-down) Triangle of 3-Triangle group, and sew in place. (One 4-Triangle group made)

Place assembled Hat flat on a table and locate the midpoint where Ear Flap will go. Turn 4-Triangle group upside down so that single (fourth) Triangle points downward away from Hat. Center 4-Triangle group on either side of Hat midpoint and sew in place.

Turn Hat over, lay it flat on a table and sew rem 4-Triangle group to second side of Hat opposite first ear flap (photo D).

5 **Crochet edging:**
RS facing, with crochet hook and desired contrast color yarn, join yarn with a slip st at lower edge of back of Hat. Ch1, work 1 sc in same space as joining slip st. Work 1 round of sc evenly spaced around entire Hat (photo E), skipping one st at each upper corner of Ear Flaps and working 3 sc into each lower point of Ear Flaps. (For Hat without Ear Flaps, simply work sc evenly spaced around entire lower edge of Hat.)

Join with a slip st to first sc. Ch1 and turn. Work 1 sc into each sc around. Join with a slip st to first sc of round. Fasten off.

Weave in ends.

◢ MAKING THE FROM-THE-TOP HAT ◣

1 Note: For Stripes, simply change colors as desired, when you run out of a color, or as the whim strikes you. You can also work this Hat in a solid color if you prefer.

Beginning at top of hat, CO 3 sts onto one dpn. Divide sts among 3 dpns, one st per needle. Place marker and join into a round, taking care not to twist sts around the needles.

Round 1: Knit, increasing in each stitch by (knit into front and back of st). (6 sts)

Round 2: Knit.

Rounds 3-4: As Round 1-2. (12 sts)

Round 5: *K1, inc in next st, rep from * around. (18 sts)

Round 6: Knit.

Round 7: *K2, inc in next st, rep from * around. (24 sts)

Round 8: Knit.

Continue in this way, adding one more st between incs on each odd round, and working all even rounds without increasing, until 37 rounds have been worked and there are 114 sts (photo A).

(Note: Switch to larger circular needle as soon as you have enough sts to fit comfortably around the circular needle.)

2 Work even in St st (knit every round) without increasing until Hat meas 1" (2.5cm) less than desired total length from top of crown, or about 6" (15cm) from beg (photo B).

Garter stitch edging:

Change to smaller circular needle.

Next Round: Purl.

Next Round: Knit.

Rep last two rounds for g st until g st section meas approx 1" (2.5cm.) BO all sts loosely.

If desired, make pompons or tassels and attach to each side of Hat at ears (photo C).

GREAT GAUNTLETS

Made with rayon-blend yarn, these gauntlets are a fun fashion accessory and look great with both casual and dressy tank tops. The cables provide a little extra stretch as well as pattern detailing.

◣ PROJECT SUMMARY ◢

Each gauntlet is worked on double-pointed needles. You'll start at the arm edge and knit a long tube, gradually decreasing as you go down the wrist. Increases at the end create the thumb gusset. Note to beginners: don't be frightened off by the cables. They're very basic and ideal for a first-timer.

◣ Designed by **CATHY CAMPBELL** ◢

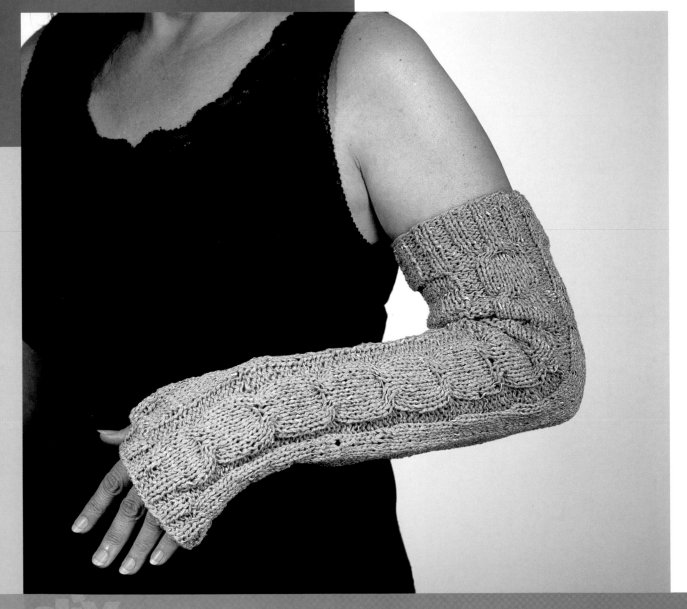

You Will Need

- Approx 112 yds/102m of a worsted-weight cotton/rayon ribbon yarn in lime
- Set of double-pointed needles in size 5 U.S. (3.75mm)
- Set of double-pointed needles in size 7 U.S. (4.5mm)
- Cable needle
- Stitch markers
- Tapestry needle

Extras

Gauge

5.5 sts = 1" (2.5cm) in St st with larger ndls

Finished Measurements

To fit average size hands. Cables allow for some stretch in finished Gauntlets.

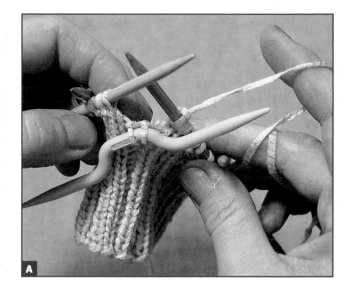

A

Rounds 2-12: Knit to first marker, p3, k8, p3, knit to end of round (photo B).

Rounds 13-84: Rep (Rounds 1-12), 6 times more. (42 sts rem)

Round 85: Knit to 1 st before first marker, k1, M1, p3, slip next 2 sts to cn and hold in back, k2, k2 from cn, slip next 2 sts to cn and hold in front, k2, k2 from cn, p3, k1, M1, knit to end of round. (44 sts)

Rounds 86-96: As Rounds 2-12.

◤ MAKING THE LEFT GAUNTLET ◥

1 **Ribbing the Gauntlet Cuff:**
With smaller dpns, CO 56 sts. Divide sts evenly among three ndls. Place marker and join to work in rounds, being careful not to twist sts around ndls.

Rib Round: *k2, p2, rep from * around.

Rep Rib Round until Gauntlet meas approx 2" (5cm) from beg.

2 **Knitting the Gauntlet Body:**
Change to larger dpns.

Setup Round: K14, place marker, p3, k8, p3, place marker, knit to end of round.

Round 1: Knit to 2 sts before first marker, sl 1 knitwise, k1, psso, p3, slip next 2 sts to cn and hold in back, k2, k2 from cn, slip next 2 sts to cn and hold in front, k2, k2 from cn, p3, k2tog, knit to end of round (photo A). (54 sts rem)

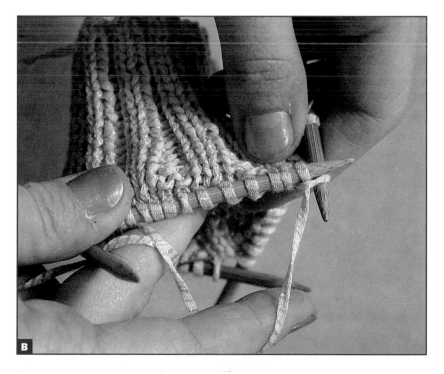

B

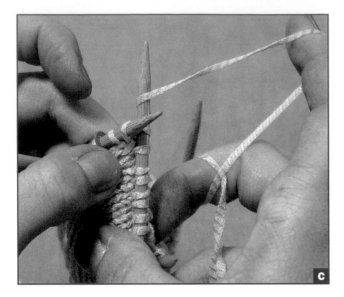

3 Making the Gauntlet Thumb Gusset (photo C):

Round 1: K1, (p1, k1) into next st, (k1, p1) into next st, knit to first marker, p3, work cables over next 8 sts as for Round 1 of Gauntlet Body, p3, knit to end of round. (46 sts)

Round 2: K1, p1, k2, p1, knit to first marker, p3, k8, p3, knit to end of round.

Round 3: K1, (p1, k1) into next st, k2, (k1, p1) into next st, knit to first marker, p3, k8, p3, knit to end of round. (48 sts)

Round 4: K1, p1, k4, p1, knit to first marker, p3, k8, p3, knit to end of round.

Round 5: K1, (p1, k1) into next st, k4, (k1, p1) into next st, knit to first marker, p3, k8, p3, knit to end of round. (50 sts)

Round 6: K1, p1, k6, p1, knit to first marker, p3, k8, p3, knit to end of round.

Round 7: K1, (p1, k1) into next st, k6, (k1, p1) into next st, knit to first marker, p3, k8, p3, knit to end of round. (52 sts)

Round 8: K1, p1, k8, p1, knit to first marker, p3, k8, p3, knit to end of round.

Round 9: K1, (p1, k1) into next st, k8, (k1, p1) into next st, knit to first marker, p3, k8, p3, knit to end of round. (54 sts)

Round 10: K1, p1, k10, p1, knit to first marker, p3, k8, p3, knit to end of round.

Round 11: K1, (p1, k1) into next st, k10, (k1, p1) into next st, knit to first marker, p3, k8, p3, knit to end of round. (56 sts)

Round 12: K1, p1, k12, knit to first marker, p3, k8, p3, knit to end of round.

Round 13: k1, (p1, k1) into next st, k12, (k1, p1) into next st, knit to first marker, p3, work cables over next 8 sts as for Round 1 of Gauntlet Body, p3, knit to end of round. (58 sts)

Round 14: K1, p1, k14, p1, knit to first marker, p3, k8, p3, knit to end of round.

Round 15: K1, (p1, k1) into next st, k14, (k1, p1) into next st, knit to first marker, p3, k8, p3, knit to end of round. (60 sts)

Round 16: K1, p1, k16, p1, knit to first marker, p3, k8, p3, knit to end of round.

4 Finishing the Gauntlet Body:

Next Round: K2, thread the 16 Gusset sts onto a scrap piece of yarn and tie loosely, knit to first marker, p3, k8, p3, knit to end of round (photo D). (44 sts)

Work even on these 44 sts, continuing to work cables on every 12th round as before, until Gauntlet meas approx 18" (45cm) from CO edge of cuff.

Change to smaller dpns.

Work Rib Round as for cuff in Step 1 until upper ribbing meas 1" (2.5cm). BO in ribbing.

5 **Finishing the Gusset:**
With smaller dpns, remove 16 Gusset sts from scrap yarn and divide as evenly as possible over 3 dpns (photo E). Place marker at inside of thumb to mark beg of rounds.

Join yarn and knit one round.

Rib Round: *K2, p2, rep from * around.

Repeat Rib Round until Ribbing meas approx 1" (2.5cm). BO all sts in ribbing.

Weave in all ends.

◀ MAKING THE RIGHT GAUNTLET ▶

6 CO 56 sts and work cuff ribbing as for Left Gauntlet.

Setup Round: P3, k8, p3, pm, k14, pm, knit to end.

Round 1: P3, slip next 2 sts to cn and hold to back, k2, k2 from cn, slip next 2 sts to cn and hold to front, k2, k2 from cn, p3, knit to 1 st after first marker, k2tog, knit to 3 sts before end of round, SSK, k1. (56 sts rem)

Rounds 2-12: P3, k8, p3, knit to end of round.

Rounds 13-84: Rep (Rounds 1-12), 6 times more. (42 sts rem)

TIPS | DIY Network Crafts

Bobby Pins as Tapestry Needles

Have you ever rushed to finish a project, but didn't have a tapestry needle handy to weave in your ends? A bobby pin works great in a pinch. Just thread the yarn through the end of the bobby pin like you would thread a needle, making sure you leave enough of a tail so the yarn doesn't slip out. Then, work as you normally would to weave the yarn through. Snip off the tail with a pair of scissors, and your project is ready to go.

E

Round 85: P3, k8, p3, knit to 1 st after first marker, M1, knit to 1 st before end of round, M1, k1. (44 sts)

7 Work Thumb Gusset as for Left Gauntlet in Step 3, except place Gusset as follows: On Round 1, p3, work Cables over next 8 sts as for Round 1 of Gauntlet Body, p3, k12, (p1, k1) into next st, (k1, p1) into next st, k to end of round. (46 sts)

Complete as for Left Gauntlet Thumb Gusset through Round 16: working 2 extra sts between each inc on every other round, and working Cables on Round 13. (60 sts)

Round 17: P3, k8, p3, k12, place 16 Gusset sts on scrap yarn holder and tie, knit to end of round. (44 sts)

8 **Finishing Right Gauntlet Body:**
Work even on these 44 sts, continuing to work cables on every 12th round as before, until Gauntlet meas approx 18" (45cm) from CO edge of cuff.

Change to smaller dpns.

Work Rib Round as for cuff until upper ribbing meas 1" (2.5cm). BO in ribbing.

Finish Thumb Gusset as for Left Gauntlet Thumb Gusset.

diy network

BEADED CUFF

Time to hand-jive baby. Even though your knitting is on fire, sometimes your wrists get cold as you work late into the night. (How many times have you said, "I'll quit after one more row."?) In order to keep the fabric flowing, make this beaded cuff to use while you knit. But once you see the bedazzling bead and lace look, you'll know the cuff is just too gorgeous to keep it to yourself—this is one project you'll want to take to the streets.

◢ PROJECT SUMMARY ◣

Our designer begins by showing you a quick and easy way for stringing beads onto the yarn using a needle and thread. With double-pointed needles, you'll make a short k2, p2 ribbed cuff before beginning the lace stitch that incorporates the beads. If you've never knit with beads, this is a great project for getting started.

◢ Designed by **CATHY CAMPBELL** ◣

Extras

Gauge

5.5 sts = 1" (2.5cm) in St st with larger ndls

Finished Measurements

Approx 7" (17.5cm) around, unstretched. Lace pattern allows Cuff to stretch to fit most wrists and lower arms.

You Will Need

Approx 112 yds/102m of a worsted-weight cotton/rayon ribbon yarn in lime

Set of double-pointed needles in size 5 U.S. (3.75mm)

Set of double-pointed needles in size 7 U.S. (4.5mm)

40 glass beads, 6mm

Sewing needle and thread

Stitch marker

Tapestry needle

◤ MAKING THE BEADED CUFF ◥

1 Pre-threading the beads:
Thread sewing needle with a fine thread. Tie thread to yarn, leaving about 3" (7.5cm) at end of yarn. Thread bead onto sewing needle and then onto yarn, pushing the bead farther down the yarn as you add beads (photo A). Continue until you have 40 beads on the yarn, making sure they are far enough down the yarn to avoid being worked in during cast-on and ribbing.

2 With smaller ndls, CO 36 sts. Divide sts evenly among three ndls. Place marker and join to work in rounds, being careful not to twist sts around ndls (photo B).

Round 1: *K5, bring yarn to front of work, sl 1 purlwise, bring down bead and hold at front of slipped st, bring yarn to back of work, k1, rep from * to end of round (photo C).

Round 2: *k4, k2tog, yo, k1, yo, sl 1 knitwise, k1, psso, rep from * to end.

Rounds 3 and 4: Knit around.

Round 5: As Round 2.

Round 6: Knit around.

Rep (Rounds 1-6), 3 times more.

Rep Round 1 once more.

Change to larger dpn's.

Rib Round: *K3, p1, rep from * around (photo D).

Rep Rib Round twice more.

BO loosely in ribbing. Weave in ends.

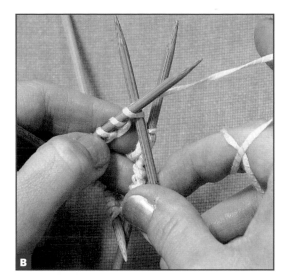

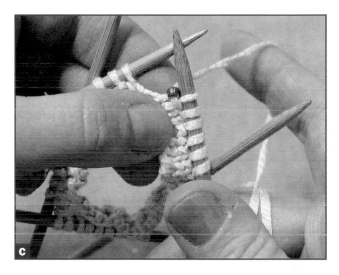

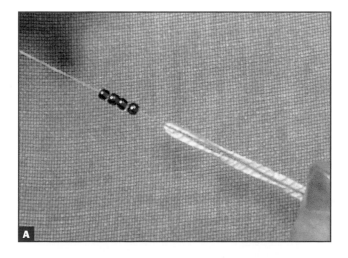

3

Home Dec & Gift Knits

Getting to the *Knitty Gritty* doesn't stop at clothing. There's so much more fun to be had knitting for the home and beyond. A cozy for your tea pot? Not in this book! How about cozies for your computer monitor and mouse? And who can live without a knit backgammon board, tailored tuxedo pillow, or journal cover? Not forgetting the classics, you'll find a teddy bear, a sampler afghan, and a lovely nine-patch baby blanket to knit as well.

BACKGAMMON BOARD

It's easy to get in the game when you can take it with you. Backgammon is one of the world's oldest games, but our designer proves it doesn't have to look like it with her contemporary use of complementary colors. And, if it isn't enough for you to roll up your board and tuck it under your arm, you can add side panels and handles to make it into an oh-so-stylish and handy tote.

◀ **PROJECT SUMARY** ▶

You'll make the board using straight needles and stockinette stitch, shaping the triangles—known as points—with short rows. The game pieces are made from I-cord that you wind into spirals and stitch. You'll felt the board and game pieces at the same time. Instructions for blocking will ensure your board is just the right size. If you want to make the board into a tote, you'll knit, felt, and attach the sides and handles.

◀ Designed by **TINA WHITMORE** ▶

You Will Need

Approx 440 yds/402m of a worsted-weight solid-color wool yarn in grass green (A)

Approx 220 yds/201m each of a worsted-weight multicolor yarn in deep pink/red mix (B), lilac/lavender mix (C), magenta/pink mix (D), and orange/deep orange mix (E).

Needles in size 10 U.S. (6mm)

Two dpns in size 10 U.S. (6mm)

Tapestry needle

Extras

Gauge

4 sts = 1" (2.5cm) in St st

Finished measurements

Board only (before felting): 13" (32.5cm) wide by 42" (105cm) long

Board only (after felting): 12" (30cm) wide by 26" (65cm) long

Special Abbreviations

yf (yarn forward): Bring working yarn to front of work as it faces you.

yb (yarn back): Bring working yarn to back of work as it faces you.

K wrap (K2 wraps): Knit wrapped st(s) tog with next st as follows: with RH needle, pick up next st, with LH needle, pick up wrap from row below and place on RH needle. Slide both sts onto LH needle and k2tog (K3tog).

P wrap (P2 wraps): Purl wrapped st(s) tog with next st as follows: with RH needle, pick up next st, with LH needle, pick up wrap from row below and place on RH needle. Slide both sts onto LH needle and p2tog tbl (P3tog tbl).

NOTES

Check measurements carefully during felting to avoid over-felting!

After felting your Board, the ends may flare to a wider width than the center. Before your Board is fully dry, stretch and pull to the correct rectangular shape.

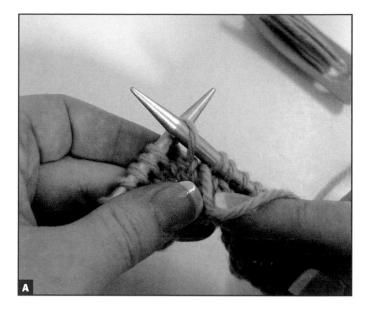

A

⬛ MAKING THE BACKGAMMON BOARD ⬛

1 With A, CO 54 sts.
Rows 1 and 3: Knit
Rows 2 and 4: Purl

2 **Begin Short Row Colorwork** (photo A):
Row 5: K48, yf, slip 1, yb, turn.
Row 6: Slip 1, p42, yb, slip 1, yf, turn.
Row 7: Slip 1, k36, yf, slip1, yb, turn.
Row 8: Slip 1, p30, yb, slip 1, yf, turn.
Row 9: Slip 1, k24, yf, slip1, yb, turn.
Row 10: Slip 1, p18, yb, slip 1, yf, turn.
Row 11: Slip 1, k12, yf, slip1, yb, turn.
Row 12: Slip 1, p6, yb, slip 1, yf, turn.

3 **Make First Pennant Shape** (photo B):
Row 13: Slip 1, k6 A, join C and *K wrap, k5, rep from * to end.
Rows 14 – 23 are worked in C as follows:
Row 14: P18, yb, slip 1, yf, turn.
Rows 15, 17, 19, 21 and 23: Slip 1, knit to end.

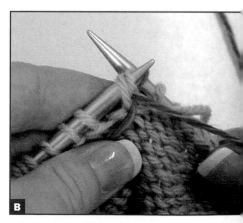

B

TIPS | DIY Network Crafts

How Much Yarn?

To figure out how much yarn to use when casting on, use this simple formula: If your pattern calls for 80 stitches, cast on 10 stitches and measure the length of the stitches. Because 10 goes into 80 eight times, multiply this length by eight to determine the total length.

Row 16: P12, yb, slip 1, yf, turn.

Row 18: P6, yb, slip 1, yf, turn.

Row 20: P6, P wrap, p5, yb, slip 1, yf, turn.

Row 22: P12, P2 wraps, p5, yb, slip 1, yf, turn.

Row 24: P18, P2 wraps, p5 with C, break yarn. P6 with A, join B and *P wrap, p5, rep from * to end.

4 Make Second Pennant Shape (photo C): **Rows 25-34 are worked in B as follows:**

Row 25: K18, yf, slip 1, yb, turn.

Rows 26, 28, 30, 32 and 34: Slip 1, purl to end.

Row 27: K12, yf, slip 1, yb, turn.

Row 29: K6, yf, slip 1, yb, turn.

Row 31: K6, K wrap, k5, yf, slip 1, yb, turn.

Row 33: K12, K2 wraps, k5, yf, slip 1, yb, turn.

Row 35: K18, K2 wraps, k5, break B, with A, k12, yf, slip 1, yb, turn.

5 Fill in Background: **Row 36:** Slip 1, P18, yb, slip 1, yf, turn.

Row 37: Slip 1, K18, K wrap, k5, yf, slip 1, yb, turn.

Row 38: Slip 1, P 24, P wrap, p5, yb, slip 1, yf, turn.

Row 39: Slip 1, K 30, K wrap, k5, yf, slip 1, yb, turn.

Row 40: Slip 1, P 36, P wrap, p5, yb, slip 1, yf, turn.

Row 41: Slip 1, K 42, K wrap, knit to end.

Row 42: P 48, P wrap, purl to end.

6 Complete First Half of Board (photo D): **Rows 43-82:** Rep Rows 3-42, using C in place of B and B in place of C.

Work (Rows 3-82), two more times.

7 Knit Center Stripe Section: Join D. Knit 2 rows.

Join E. Knit 2 rows.

Knit 2 more rows in D.

Knit 2 more rows in E.

Knit 2 more rows in D.

8 Complete Second Half of Board: Work (Rows 3-82), three more times.

With A, work (Rows 1-4), once more.

BO with A.

◣ MAKING THE GAME PIECES ◢

9 With D or E and dpn, CO 4 sts. Knit one row. For I-cord, do not turn. Slide sts to opposite end of needle. Bring yarn around back of work to beg next row. Rep this procedure until I-cord meas approx 7" (17.5cm) from beg. BO. Weave in I-cord ends. Make 15 I-cords each in both D and E.

◣ FELTING THE BOARD AND GAME PIECES ◢

10 Set your washing machine to hot and use a heavy-duty cycle with low water. Add the game board and I-cords after the agitation cycle begins. Repeat agitation cycle as necessary to achieve full felting and desired size, but do not let pieces go through the spin cycle. Keep a close eye on size to avoid over-shrinking. When the sts disappear and the pieces are stiff, you have successfully felted them! Squeeze the pieces in a towel and dry flat on a hard surface, stretching to desired shape and size while still damp.

11 After felting, I-cords will shrink to about 6" (15cm) long. Wind each I-cord into a flat spiral. Tack securely into circular shape (photo E).

◣ OPTIONAL TOTE BAG FINISHING ◢

12 **Side Panels (Make 2):**
With straight ndls and D, CO 60 sts. Knitting every row, repeat Step 6 of Board instructions for center stripe section. BO.

13 **Straps (Make 2):**
Work as for Side Panels.
NOTE: Felt Straps and Side Panels before attaching to Board edges to ensure accurate sizing.
Sew CO edge of each Side Panel to center stripe section of Board. Fold Board in half and sew side edges of each Side Panel to each half of Board.
Sew both ends of one Strap to one side of finished tote bag, a few inches down from the opening at the top, and spaced a few inches apart. Repeat for second Strap, attaching to opposite side of bag so that it lines up with first Strap.

14 **Closure Buttons:**
Make and felt one Game Piece in D. Sew into a spiral shape and attach to front side of tote bag between Straps to make a button for closure. Make and felt another Game Piece in E. Attach to tote on opposite top edge, forming a loop above top of bag. Fold loop down to opposite side and close loop around button.

OPTIONAL TOTE BAG FINISHING

SAMPLER AFGHAN

We invited some of the hippest moms and grandmas we know to our show to knit the blocks for this sampler. While you could call it a family affair, you'll never call this afghan quaint. The contemporary color scheme, combined with some of the best heirloom techniques we love, make this project a bit of knitting history that will fit right into even the most mod room.

Designed by
BETSY MCCALL

◣ **PROJECT SUMMARY** ◢

Making a sampler is a great way to learn new patterns. It's also great for knitters on the go. Because you make each block separately to seam together later, you can knit them during your commute, at lunch, or while waiting just about anywhere. For this project you'll make blocks of honeycomb cable, loop, eyelet, bramble, and hurdle stitches, as well as some old standbys like the stockinette, rib, and garter stitches. Once you seam the blocks together, you'll crochet around the edges and add decorative tassels to the corners.

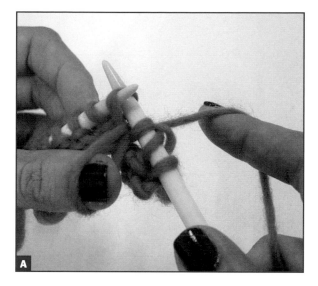

A

You Will Need

Approx 327 yds/300m each of a chunky-weight wool yarn in bright orange (A), fuchsia (B), and light pink (C)

Approx 1090 yds/1000m of a chunky-weight wool yarn in red/pink mix (D)

1 pair needles in size 10 U.S. (6mm)

Crochet hook, size K/10.5 (6.5mm)

Tapestry needle

Extras

Gauge

3 sts = 1" (2.5cm) in g st (knit every row)

Finished Measurements

48" (120cm) square (not including crochet edging)

◣ **MAKING THE GARTER STITCH SQUARES** ◢

1 **Garter Stitch Square (Make 11):**
With D, CO 24 sts.
Knit every row until Garter Stitch Square meas approx 8" (20cm) (20cm) from beg. BO loosely.

2 **Loopy Square (Make 4):**
With A, CO 24 sts.
Row 1: K2, *(k1, but keep st on LH needle, with yarn in front, wrap yarn around thumb, with yarn in back, knit original st again, this time letting it fall from needle (photo A). Pass the 2nd st on the RH needle over the first st), k1, rep from * to end.
Rep Row 1 until Loopy Square meas approx 8" (20cm) from beg. BO loosely.
NOTE: You can vary the size of the loops by holding your thumb farther away from the needle, or by wrapping the yarn around your thumb more than once.

3 **Lace Square (Make 4):**
With A, CO 24 sts.
Row 1: K1, *yo, SSK, rep from * to last st, k1 (photo B, following page).
Rep Row 1 until Lace Square meas approx 8" (20cm) from beg. BO loosely.

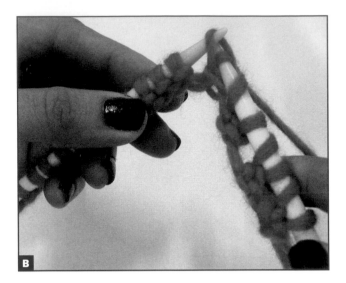

4 **Hurdle Stitch Square (Make 4):**
With C, CO 28 sts.
Rows 1-2: Knit.
Rows 3-4: *K1, p1, rep from * to end.
Rep Rows 1-4 until Hurdle Stitch Square meas approx 8" (20cm) from beg. BO loosely.

5 **Checkerboard Square (Make 4):**
With C, CO 28 sts.
Rows 1-5: K7, p7, k7, p7.
Rows 6-10: P7, k7, p7, k7.
Rep Rows 1-10 until Checkerboard Square meas approx 8", ending with a Row 5 or Row 10. BO loosely.

6 **Popcorn Square (Make 4):**
With B, CO 23 sts.
Row 1: With C, knit.
Row 2: With C, knit.
Rows 3, 5: With B, knit.
Rows 4, 6: With B, purl.
Row 7: With C, k1, *drop next st down to the last C row, insert needle in loop of C st and under the four unraveled threads of C and knit the st, k3, rep from * to last st, k1 (photo C).
Row 8: With C, purl.
Rows 9, 11: With B, knit.

TIPS | DIY Network
Crafts

Switching Needles

If you're just learning to knit, there's a good chance you may be casting on too tightly, making it almost impossible to knit the first row without sliding the stitches to the very tip of the needle. Try casting on with a smaller-sized needle (like a dpn) held together with the needle you intend to work with. Then, when ready to knit the first row, just slide out the small needle. You'll end up with a nice, neat cast on row that's much easier to work with.

Rows 10, 12: With B, purl.

Row 13: With C, k3, *drop next st down to the last C row, insert needle in loop of C st and under the four unraveled threads of C, and knit the st, k3, rep from * to last st, k1.

Row 14: With C, purl.

Rep Rows 3-14 until Popcorn Square meas approx 8" (20cm) from beg. BO loosely.

Work second Popcorn Square as above, switching colors B and C. (See photo D for detailed view.)

Work 2 more Popcorn Squares as above, using B only.

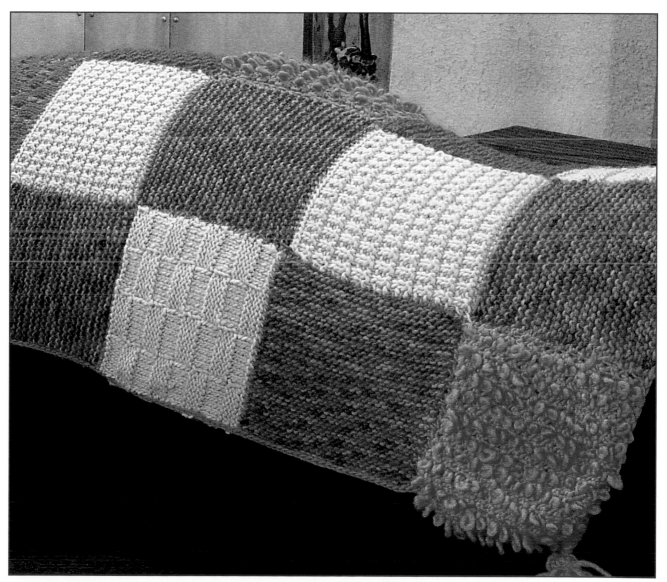

Knit Bits:
COOL TOOLS

◣ Bamboo Needles ◢

Cotton yarn and aluminum needles—they mix together about as well as water and oil. Use bamboo needles in these cases; they have a slight texture that keeps the cotton from slipping off.

◣ Pull Ball ◢

Has winding yarn ever given you a skein in the neck? Wind that pain away with this knitter's little helper — a prescription pill bottle. Simply pop the cap and relief is on its way. Slip the end of the yarn inside the bottle, replace the cap, and begin winding. Before you know it, you'll have a perfectly wound center pull ball, and no more headaches!

◣ Yarn Measurer ◢

If someone gives you a few unmarked balls of yarn and you need to know much is there, simply wind the yarn around an 18" piece of cardboard and count the number of strands shown on the board. Each strand represents one yard.

◣ Kitschy Stitch Markers ◢

Have you super-sized your knitting needles, but not your stitch markers? Try using a kitschy key chain instead. The variety is endless, and it adds pizzazz to any work in progress!

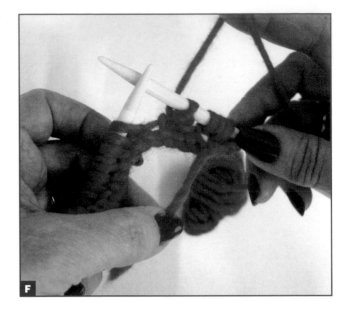

F

7 **Bramble Stitch Square (Make 4):**
With B, CO 30 sts.
Row 1 (RS): Purl.
Row 2 (WS): K1, *(k1, p1, k1) into next st, p3tog, rep from * to last st, k1 (photo F).
Row 3: Purl.
Row 4: K1, *p3tog, (k1, p1, k1) into next st, rep from * to last st, k1.
Rep Rows 1-4 until Bramble Stitch Square meas approx 8" (20cm) from beg. BO loosely.

◣ FINISHING THE SAMPLER AFGHAN ◢

8 Arrange the squares in a pleasing pattern, 7 blocks wide and 5 blocks tall. Using tapestry ndl and matching color yarn, sew squares tog into a column, then sew assembled columns tog.

9 Using desired edging color and crochet hook, join yarn with a slip st at any corner of assembled afghan. Ch1, work 1 round of single crochet evenly spaced around entire perimeter of afghan, working 3 sc into each corner. Join with a slip st to first sc. If desired, work further rounds of crochet including decorative sts of your choice. Cut yarn. Fasten off. Weave in all ends.

◢ PROJECT SUMMARY ◣

This throw features a classic combination of
stitch variations. Each square has a distinct look,
but the unifying use of seed stitch variations
creates an overall visual symmetry. The blocks
include simple seed stitches, the seed stitch
check, and a honeycomb cable that's bordered
with seed stitches. A crocheted pecot border
adds a decorative touch.

Designed by
◢ LIBBY BAILEY & VICKIE HOWELL ◣

FAMILY HEIRLOOM THROW

In addition to being a great way to learn new stitches, samplers are also the ideal project for collabora-
tions. The blocks in this throw were made separately
by mother-daughter knitters who live far apart.
During their next visit, they assembled the blocks
and added the edging, creating cherished memories
and a special heirloom.

You Will Need

Approx 355 yds/320m bulky weight in color A

Approx 355 yds/320m bulky weight in color B

Knitting needles appropriate for yarn choice (see yarn label)

Cable needle

Crochet hook appropriate for yarn choice

Tapestry needle

Safety pins

Extras

Gauge

Gauge is not critical; it will depend on your yarn choice.

Finished measurements

Finished block measurement approx 7" x 7" (18 cm)

Finished afghan size approx 28" x 35" (71 x 89 cm)

Special Abbreviations

C4B: Slip next 2 sts onto cable needle and hold at back of the work, knit next 2 sts from the left-hand needle, then knit the 2 sts from the cable needle.

C4F: Slip next 2 sts onto cable needle and hold at front of the work, knit next 2 sts from left-hand needle, then knit the 2 sts from the cable needle.

Stitch Patterns

Honeycomb Cable Stitch Pattern
Row 1 (RS): *C4B, C4F; rep from * to end.
Row 2 (and all even rows): Purl.
Row 3: Knit.
Row 5: *C4F, C4B; rep from * to end.
Row7: Knit.
Row 8: Purl.
Repeat these 8 rows.

Seed Stitch Pattern
Row 1: K1, p1; rep to end.
Row 2: P1, k1; rep to end.

Seed Stitch Check Pattern
Row 1 (RS): K5, *(p1, k1) twice, p1, k5; rep from * to end.
Row 2: P6, *k1, p1, k1, p7; rep from* to last 9 sts, k1, p1, k1, p6.
Row 3: Rep Row 1.
Row 4: Rep Row 2.
Row 5: Rep Row 1.
Row 6: *(k1, p1) twice, k1, p5; rep from* to last 5 sts, (k1, p1) twice, k1.
Row 7: (k1, p1) twice, k7, p1, k1, p1; rep from* to last st, k1.
Row 8: Rep Row 6.
Row 9: Rep Row 7.
Row 10: Rep Row 6.
Repeat these 10 rows.

A

MAKING THE SQUARES

1 **Honeycomb Cable Stitch Squares (Make 8):**
With Color B, CO 30 sts. Work 3 rows in seed stitch (photo A).

Follow stitch pattern (photos B and C), keeping a seed stitch border on first three and last three stitches of each row. Repeat 8 row stitch pattern (including seed stitch border) 6 times.

Work 2 rows of seed stitch. BO in seed stitch.

2 **Seed Stitch Squares (Make 6):**
With Color B, CO 36 sts. Work in stitch pattern until piece measures 7" (18 cm). BO.

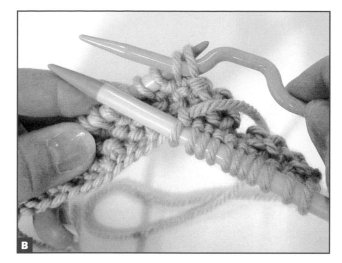

3 **Seed Stitch Check Squares (Make 6):**
With Color A, CO 25 sts. Work in stitch pattern until piece measures 7" (18cm). BO.

◢ FINISHING ◣

4 Arrange squares in pleasing pattern, pinning together with safety pins. Using tapestry needle and mattress stitch, sew blocks together, taking care not to pucker the seams.

◢ PICOT CROCHETED BORDER ◣

5 Using Color A and beg on a corner edge of the blanket, sc around entire piece (photo D). Turn. *Ch 4, sl st into base of ch, sc 3, rep from * to end (photo E).

TIPS | DIY Network Crafts

Colored point protectors
If you're forced to put your knitting down mid-row, use different colored point protectors so you'll always know which needle belongs in your right hand. Try using red for right; it's easy to remember.

PRETTY PILLOWS

Forget formality—these pillows are all about fun. Whether your home is urban chic, classic French country, or somewhere in between, these schemes will lend a bit of frivolity to any room. If you worry about keeping the pillow pristine, the buttoned-up back lets you easily remove the pillow form to clean the cover as needed.

◢ **PROJECT SUMMARY** ◣

Both pillows are knitted identically, using the Basic Pillow instructions. Each Pillow Back is made in two parts which are later buttoned together. After you seam the front and back pieces together, you'll sew buttons covered in grosgrain ribbon on the back to add the finishing touch.

◢ Designed by **ALLISON WHITLOCK** ◣

You Will Need

Fleur-de-Lis Pillow:

Approx 428 yds/392m of a light worsted-weight wool yarn in wine (A)

Approx 214 yds/196m of a light-weight wool yarn in cherry red (B)

¼ yd (22.5cm) of wide cherry-colored grosgrain ribbon

½ yd (45cm) of tear-away stabilizer

56" (140cm) of cotton piping cord

Tuxedo Pillow:

Approx 410 yds/375m of a light-weight wool yarn in black (A)

Approx 546 yds/500m of a light-weight wool yarn in cream (B)

¼ yd (22.5cm) of wide cream or off-white grosgrain ribbon

Both Pillows:

Needles in size 6 U.S. (4mm)

3 self-cover buttons

14" (35cm) square pillow form

Sewing needle and pins

Tapestry needle

Extras

Gauge for Both Pillows

23 sts and 31 rows = 4" (10cm) in St st

Finished measurements

14" (35cm) square, not including edgings.

MAKING THE BASIC PILLOW

1 First Half of Pillow Back:
With A, CO 80 sts.

Work in St st until piece meas approx 7" (17.5cm) from beg, ending with a WS row.

2 Buttonhole Placement:
Knit 4 rows.

Next Row (RS): K20, BO 4 sts, k14, BO 4 sts, k14 (photo A), BO 4 sts, knit to end.

Next Row (WS): K20, *turn work, CO 4 sts, turn work, k14, rep from * two times more, knit to end.
Knit 4 rows.
BO.

3 Second half of Pillow Back:
With A, CO 80 sts.

Work in St st until piece meas approx 7" (17.5cm) from beg, ending with a WS row.
Knit 10 rows.
BO.

4 Pillow Front:
With A for Fleur-de-Lis Pillow and B for Tuxedo Pillow, CO 80 sts.

Work in St st until Pillow Front meas approx 14" (35cm) from beg, ending with a WS row.
BO.

FINISHING THE FLEUR-DE-LIS PILLOW

1 Applique square:
With B, CO 60 sts.

Work in g st (knit every row) until applique piece meas approx 10" (25cm) square. BO.

2 Knit Piping:
With B, CO 12 sts.

Work in g st (knit every row) until Piping meas approx 56" (140cm). BO.

Fold your knitting for piping around cotton piping cord to create a thin sausage shape (photo B, next page). Pin and sew in place by hand or by machine, as desired.

Using sewing machine, or a very small running st by hand, sew around the fleur-de-lis shape of the template. Tear away stabilizer (photo D).

Turn Pillow Front to RS and cut away knitted pillow front fabric inside your sewn sts, revealing the Applique beneath. Allow edges to curl and fray a little (photo E).

3 Using Illustration A, trace pattern onto a 10" (25cm) square piece of tear-away stabilizer. Pin Applique Square to WS of Pillow Front, with stabilizer on top (photo C).

Illustration A: Fleur-de-Lis Template
(enlarge 260%)

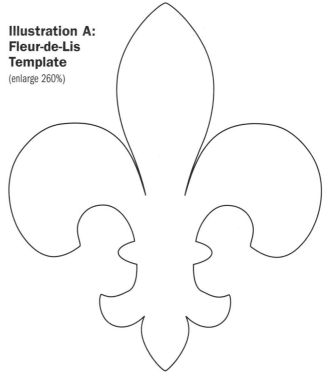

4 Weave in all ends. Cover buttons with grosgrain ribbon according to manufacturer's instructions.

Stitch buttons in place on button band of second half of Pillow Back, lining up buttons with buttonholes on first half of Pillow Back. (photo F)

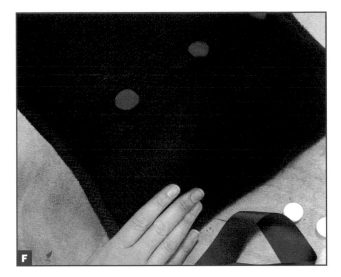

5 Press and block all Pillow pieces. Leaving buttonhole edge open, hold Front and Back pieces tog with their right sides facing each other. Place piping between the seams and backstitch all pieces tog.

Turn Pillow to RS and insert pillow form.

◀ FINISHING THE TUXEDO PILLOW ▶

1 **Tuxedo Ruffles (Make 5):**
With A, CO 160 sts.

Row 1: Knit.

Row 2: With B, knit.

Rows 3-7: With B, work in St st, beg with a knit row.

Row 8: With B, *k2tog, rep from * to end (photo A). (80 sts rem)

Row 9: With B, purl.

Row 10: *K into front and back of next st, rep from * to end. (160 sts)

Rows 11-16: With B, work in St st, beg with a purl row.

Row 17: With A, Knit.

BO with A.

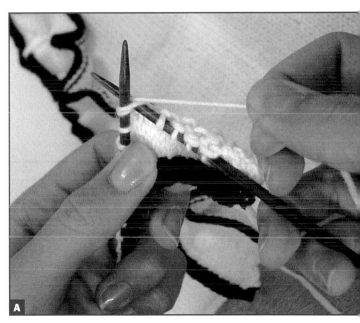

2 Weave in all ends. Press and block all Pillow pieces.

Pin Tuxedo Ruffles to Pillow Front and hand sew to Front with a running st or a series of cross-stitches along the center of each Ruffle (photo B).

Cover buttons and stitch in place to Pillow Back following instructions for Step 4 of Fleur-de-Lis Pillow finishing.

Leaving buttonhole edges open, hold Front and Back pieces tog with their right sides facing each other. Backstitch pieces tog.

Turn Pillow to RS and insert Pillow form.

SUNBURST JOURNAL COVER

Hey, sunshine! How 'bout grabbing a few rays? Put some solar energy into your journaling with this great knit cover. Entrelac—an easy technique for making a basket-weave pattern—creates the sunburst motif. With a few added tips on how to cover your book, you'll have a custom journal in no time—without getting sunburned.

◀ PROJECT SUMMARY ▶

You'll make the motif first, beginning with knitting eight triangles together on straight needles. Then you'll switch to double-pointed needles to work in the round to complete the design. Using stockinette stitch, you'll knit the jacket cover in one piece, shaping the flaps as you work. Then you'll cover the book and sew on the motif. Hint: This would make a hot gift for any journaler!

◀ Designed by **CECILY KEIM** ▶

You Will Need

Approx 300 yds/275m of a worsted-weight cotton yarn in sage green (A)

Approx 50 yds/46m each of a worsted-weight cotton yarn in bright orange (B) and lavender (C)

Needles in size 7 U.S. (4.5mm)

9 dpns in size 7 U.S. (4.5mm)

Tapestry needle

Hardbound or wirebound journal book, 8½" by 11" (21.25cm by 27.5cm)

Desired fabric for lining

Extras

Finished measurements

Sunburst Motif: 10" square (25cm square)

Book Cover: 11" (27.5cm) tall by 18½" (46.25cm) wide

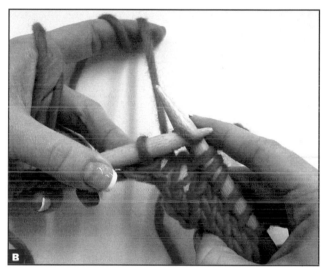

MAKING THE ENTRELAC SUNBURST MOTIF

1 NOTE: You will create 8 base triangles, each worked over 6 sts.

With B and straight ndls, CO 48 sts.

First Tier:

Work first triangle as follows:

Row 1: K2, turn.

Row 2: Slip 1, p1, turn.

Row 3: Slip 1, k2, turn (photo A).

Row 4: Slip 1, p2, turn.

Row 5: Slip 1, k3, turn.

Row 6: Slip 1, p3, turn.

Row 7: Slip 1, k4, turn.

Row 8: Slip 1, p4, turn.

Row 9: Slip 1, k5, turn.

Row 10: Slip 1, p5, turn.

Row 11: Slip 1, k5, do not turn.

Leaving last sts worked on RH needle, *Rep Rows 1-11 over next sts from LH needle (photo B). Rep from * until 8 triangles have been worked.

Leaving a tail, cut yarn.

2 Transfer each triangle separately to a dpn, so that each triangle rests on its own needle (photo C, previous page). Use the CO tail to tie the two end triangles tog at their bottom tips. You will now begin working in the round, using the free dpn to begin.

3 Second Tier:
This tier creates rectangles in the spaces between triangles.

Work the first rectangle:

Row 1: With C and WS facing, using empty dpn, purl across sts of first triangle, then pick up and purl 5 sts along side of first triangle. (To pick up and purl, insert needle from back to front into desired space, then wrap yarn around needle purlwise from the front and pull this wrap through the same space to the back.) Turn.

Row 2: Using the needle holding triangle sts to your right, slip 1, k4, turn.

Row 3: Using an empty needle, slip 1, p3, p2 tog, turn. (You will be purling tog one st from your working needle and 1 st from the next triangle.)

Rep Rows 2-3 until all of the sts from the next triangle have been worked.

Next Row: Slip 1, k4, turn.

Next Row: Slip 1, p4, turn.

Continue to work rectangles as above, working one rectangle into each triangle space across the round (photo D).

4 Third Tier:
This tier creates a rectangle along the side of each previous rectangle.

Row 1: With C and RS facing, Slip 1, knit across sts just worked on first needle. Pick up and knit 8 sts along side edge of next rectangle. Turn.

Row 2: Using the needle holding sts to your right, slip 1, p7, turn.

Row 3: Using an empty needle, slip 1, k6, SSK, turn.

Repeat Rows 2-3 until all of the sts from the next rectangle have been worked.

Next Row: Slip 1, p7, turn.

Next Row: Slip 1, k7, turn.

Next Row: Slip 1, p7, turn.

Next Row: Slip 1, k7, turn.

BO. Cut yarn.

For subsequent rectangles, join a separate strand of C. Continue to work rectangles as above, working one rectangle into side of each rectangle across the round (photo E). BO.

◀ MAKING THE BOOK JACKET ▶

NOTE: You will start with the two bottom flaps, working the two pieces at the same time. To do this, simply CO for each piece on the same needles, using a separate ball of yarn to work each piece.

5 With A and straight ndls, CO 26. With separate strand of A, CO 26 onto same needle.

Row 1: Knit across first 26 sts, drop yarn, pick up second strand of yarn and knit across rem 26 sts.

Rows 2-13: Purl across, changing yarns midway as before.

Continue in St st over both pieces until 13 rows have been worked.

Row 14 (WS): Purl 26. Cut first strand of yarn. With second strand of yarn, p26, then CO 15 sts at end of row.

Rows 15-81 (RS): Knit 41. With same strand of yarn, CO 7 sts at center of row, then cont with same strand of yarn across rem 26 sts, then CO 15 sts at end of row. The two pieces are now joined and there are a total of 89 sts. Cont in St st across all 89 sts until 81 rows total have been worked from CO row.

Row 82 (WS): BO 15 sts, purl 26, drop yarn. Join a second ball of yarn and BO center 7 sts, purl to end of row.

Row 83 (RS): BO 15 sts, knit 26. With second ball of yarn, knit across rem 26 sts.

Cont in St st, working both sides at same time with separate balls of yarn as before, until 98 rows total have been worked from CO row.

BO all sts of both pieces.

◀ PUTTING IT ALL TOGETHER ▶

6 Block the book jacket so that the flaps are folded and creased, using a steam iron (photo F). Following the photos, pin the ends of the flaps around Journal as shown and sew in place (photo G).

7 Place the Entrelac Sunburst Motif on the front of the Book Jacket and whipstitch in place.

8 Cut fabric to fit size of front and back of journal cover. Using the photo as a guide, sew fabric pieces to the flaps on the inside of the Journal (photo H).

TEDDY SWEATER

Sure, it looks sweet and cute on teddy now. But Knitsters, be aware that making this teeny, fair-isle sweater takes knitting nerves of steel. On the show, our designer showed us steeking, the traditional Scottish method of cutting—yes, cutting—the knit fabric for setting the sleeves and making the shoulder seams. When you're finished, you'll not only have a cuddly teddy sweater, you'll have the skill to try this technique on larger fair-isle projects. Ready? Dare you!

◤ PROJECT SUMMARY ◥

By following these great step-by-step instructions you'll overcome any anxiety about cutting fair isle knits. Really, the stitches won't unravel. Using circular needles and the stockinette stitch you'll knit the body. (Remember, on circular needles that means knit every round—how easy is that?) Then you'll knit the sleeves, also on circular needles. You'll measure carefully, mark, then use a sewing machine to stitch boundaries that create the guidelines for cutting the fabric. After cutting the fabric you'll sew the shoulder seams and set in the sleeves using a tapestry needle and yarn.

◤ Designed by **KAREN BAUMER** ◥

You Will Need

- Approx 110 yds/100m each of a sport-weight wool yarn in sage green (MC) and cream (CC)
- 1 set dpns in size 2 U.S. (2.75mm)
- 1 set dpns in size 3 U.S. (3.25mm)
- Tapestry needle
- Stitch markers
- Steam iron
- Sharp scissors
- Sewing machine

Extras

Gauge:

6.25 sts = 1" (2.5cm) and 7.25 rows = 1" (2.5cm) in St st, worked in the round in chart patt

Finished measurements:

Chest: 13" (32.5cm) around

Length: 5" (12.5cm)

This size will fit a 13" tall (32.5cm) teddy bear with approx 9" (22.5cm) torso circumference.

Body Chart

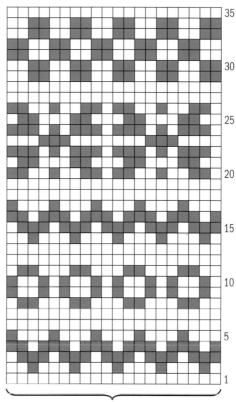

20 St Repeat

Sleeve Chart

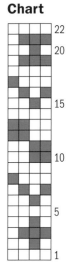

4 St Repeat

Key

☐ = MC

▨ = CC

◢ MAKING THE SWEATER ◣

1 **Body:** With MC and smaller dpns, CO 80 sts. Place marker and join to work in the round, being careful not to twist sts. Work in St st (knit every round) for 5 rounds. Purl one round for turning ridge.
Change to larger dpns and work one round even.

2 Work 35 rounds following Body chart, stranding color not in use loosely across WS of work (photo A).
Purl one round.
BO knitwise, keeping marker at beg of round and placing a second marker after 40 sts. These markers indicate the side seams of the sweater.

3 **Sleeves:** (Make 2) With MC and smaller dpns, CO 44 sts. Join and work in the round

A

but lower it straight down, then lift straight up. With pieces still inside out, place one Sleeve along side edge of Body at one of the marked seams. Sleeve should be perpendicular to Body, just as it will be after sewing (photo B). Mark Sleeve depth with a pin or a stitch marker.

Repeat on other side for second Sleeve.

5 Prepare Sleeve openings:
Set sewing machine to a straight stitch, about 12 sts per inch (2.5 cm). Mark the column of sts on the Body which runs straight down from the marker at the top edge to the point where you marked the Sleeve depth. In the column of sts just next to that center column, stitch with the sewing machine down the center of that column to the marked point (photo C). Pivot and stitch across the marked column and into the center of the column just next to it on the other side. Pivot and stitch back up to the top edge. Stitch one more time over your existing stitches.

Knit Bits:
BLOOMING YARN

Blooming refers to a yarn's tendency to puff up and become fuller when washed and dried. In this way, yarn is kind of like hair. If you take someone with really curly hair and you brush it, pull it, and fuss with it, the hair will eventually straighten. But, once their hair gets wet again, it's going to snap back into its curly natural state. With yarns, the fibers have been combed, spun, and plied into yarn. But when you get the yarn wet, those fibers will try to return to their natural shape—just like curly hair. That's why whenever you knit something that you intend to wash, it's important to knit a gauge swatch and then wash it to see how the yarn is going to react. Measure your swatch after it has dried and adjust your gauge accordingly.

as for Body of sweater for 5 rounds. Purl one round for turning ridge.

Change to larger dpns.

Work 22 rounds following Sleeve chart, stranding color not in use loosely across WS of work.

Purl 5 rounds for inner Sleeve top facing.

BO purlwise.

◄ FINISHING THE SWEATER ►

4 Turn Body and Sleeves inside out. Weave in all ends. Block pieces lightly from WS, using steam iron and applying very slight pressure. To prevent accidental felting, do not move iron against pieces,

Repeat on second side of Body for rem Sleeve opening.

6 With scissors, cut open the fabric along the marked column, between the vertical rows of machine stitching you made (photo D). This will create front and back flaps.

Place BO edges of Body tog, WS facing you. With MC and tapestry needle, whipstitch the shoulder seams tog through the purl bumps of the last row (photo E).

7 Turn pieces right side out. Insert a Sleeve into a Sleeve opening so that the first purl row of the upper Sleeve facing is visible, but the remaining part of the facing is stuffed inside the Sleeve opening. Pin Sleeve in place (photo F).

With MC and tapestry needle, sew Sleeve into opening, attaching the visible purl row of the Sleeve to the first stitch on the Body outside the machine stitching. Be sure to work into this same column of Body stitches all the way around the opening for a neat seam.

8 When both Sleeves are sewn in, turn garment inside out. Lightly sew down the Sleeve top facings over the raw edges that were created by cutting the Body. Fold up the bottom facings of the Body and Sleeves along the purled turning ridges and sew lightly in place (photo G).

COMPUTER COZIES

Gather around Knitsters, the world is full of items just waiting to be cozied. These great geek-chic knits will transform your cold computer into a warm and whimsical work station. The lion monitor cover and mouse cozy will put you in a good mood every time you sit down and log on—even when you're doing taxes and paying bills. Made by working the stockinette stitch and using a few simple shaping techniques, this project is great for beginners and makes a wonderful gift.

◢ PROJECT SUMMARY ◣

You'll make the mouse cozy in three parts, starting with the tail, then the football-shaped body, and finally the head, which is sewn on later. For the body, you'll work the stocknette stitch with straight needles. For the monitor cover, you'll use circular needles, shaping the corners by decreasing to create a mitered fit. Each ear is made with a furry inside and smooth outside that you knit separately then sew together. The lion's tail is optional—but who can resist?

◢ Designed by **BETSY MCCALL** ◣

You Will Need

Mouse Cozy:

Approx 140 yds/128m of a chunky-weight brushed wool-blend yarn in charcoal (A)

Approx 80 yds/73m of a chunky-weight acrylic blend ribbon tape yarn in black (B)

1 yard/1m of a fine-weight polyester eyelash yarn in white for whiskers

Straight ndls in size 9 U.S. (5.5mm)

1 set of dpns in size 9 U.S. (5.5mm)

Monitor Cozy:

Approx 56 yds/51m of a bulky-weight wool-blend eyelash yarn ("fur-type") in brown/tan mix (A)

Approx 56 yds/51m of a bulky-weight polyester "fur-type yarn" in matching brown/tan mix (B)

Approx 100 yds/91m of a fine-weight, space-dyed, eyelash yarn in variegated browns (C)

Approx 109 yds/100m of a bulky-weight smooth wool yarn in oatmeal (D)

Approx 97 yds/89m of a bulky-weight microfiber eyelash yarn in white (E)

Circular ndl in size 17 U.S. (13mm), 29" (72.5cm) long

Straight ndls in size 13 U.S. (9mm), 9" (22.5cm) long

1 set dpns in size 13 U.S. (9mm)

Both Projects:

Tapestry needle

Extras

Gauges

Mouse Cozy: 3.75 sts = 1" (2.5cm)

Monitor Cozy: Body: 1 st = 1" (2.5cm),
Ears & Tail: 2.5 sts = 1" (2.5cm)

Finished measurements

To fit average sized mouse and a 17" (42.5cm) CRT monitor (Note: the finished piece has a fair amount of stretch to it and works for a range of monitor sizes.)

⬛ **MAKING THE MOUSE COZY** ⬛

1 Making the tail: With dpns and A, CO 3 sts (photo A). For I-cord, do not turn work, but slide sts to opposite end of needle. Pull yarn behind work to beg knitting next row. Work I-cord in this manner until tail meas approx 4" (10cm) from beg, ending with a WS row.

2 Shape Lower Body:
Row 1: K3.
Row 2: CO 5 sts at beg of row, p8. (8 sts)
Rows 3-4: CO 5 sts at beg of row 3, then work 2 rows even in St st, turning at end of each row. (13 sts)
Row 5: K5, k into front and back loop of next st, k1, k into front and back loop of next st, k5. (15 sts)
Row 6: Purl across.

Rep Rows 5-6, increasing as before, until there are 21 sts on needle (photo B, previous page).

Work even in St st until piece meas approx 4" (10cm) from beg of Lower Body, not including tail, ending with a WS row.

3 Upper Body:
Row 1: K8, k2tog tbl, k1, ktog, k8. (19 sts)
Row 2: P7, p2tog tbl, k1, p2tog, p7. (17 sts)

Row 3: K2, k2tog tbl, k2, k2tog tbl, k1, k2tog, k2, k2tog, k2. (13 sts)
Row 4: P2, p2tog tbl, p2tog tbl, k1, p2tog, p2tog, p1. (9 sts)
BO all sts (photo C).

◄ MAKING THE MOUSE HEAD ►

4 Beg at back of Head, with straight ndls or dpns and A, CO 33 sts.
Row 1: Knit.
Row 2: Purl.
Row 3: K9, k2tog tbl, k11, k2tog, k9 (31 sts).
Rows 4, 6, 8, 10, 12, 14, 16: Purl.
Row 5: K8, k2tog tbl, k11, k2tog, k8. (29 sts).
Row 7: K7, k2tog tbl, k11, k2tog, k7. (27 sts).
Row 9: K6, k2tog tbl, k11, k2tog, k6. (25 sts).
Row 11: K5, k2tog tbl, k11, k2tog, k5. (23 sts).
Row 13: k4, k2tog tbl, k3, k2tog tbl, k1, k2tog, k3, k2tog, k4 (19 sts) (photo D).

Knit Bits:
POLYMER CLAY POINT PROTECTORS

Accidents happen — and sometimes (take a deep breath) they can happen to your knitting! But not all accidents have to end in catastrophe. A set of point protectors will keep your latest project on the needles should anything unforeseen happen. Polymer clay is a perfect material for making your own stylish point protectors. All you do is break off a chunk of the clay, roll it into a ball, press the point of your needle into the ball, and wiggle it around slightly to get the hole just right. Then bake the clay (with the needles removed) according to the manufacturer's instructions and—ta da! Cool point protectors you can say you made yourself!

Row 15: K3, k2tog tbl, k2, k2tog tbl, k1, k2tog, k2, k2tog, k3. (15 sts)

Row 17: K2, k2tog tbl, k1, k2tog tbl, k1, k2tog, k1, k2tog, k2. (11 sts)

BO 11 sts.

5 **Finishing the Mouse Head:** Roll the triangle you've just made into an ice cream cone shape. Sew the long edges tog (photo E). This seam will be under the chin of the mouse's head. Using small bits of yarn, stuff the nose, making a round snout. Stuff skull with yarn clippings in the same way, rounding it out as desired. Sew the center 5 or 6 sts of top of Head to the bottom of Head. Let the corner sts curl out to become ears. Pinch ears toward front of Mouse Head and tack tog in this position. Mold head with fingers until desired shape is achieved.

FINISHING THE MOUSE

6 Using ribbon yarn and tapestry needle, embroider black nose close to the tip of the nose. Embroider eyes two-thirds of the way down the face, close to the nose. The bigger the eyes and the smaller the nose, the cuter your Mouse will be! With white eyelash yarn, add whiskers by sewing or attaching fringe to either side of the nose.

Sew the Head to the Body.

Weave in ends.

MAKING THE MONITOR COZY MANE

1 With circular ndl, holding A, B, and C tog as one yarn, CO 68 sts. Place marker and join in rounds, being careful not to twist sts around needle. Knit every round until Mane meas approx 5" (12.5cm) from beg. (photo A)

2 **Shape corners:**
Round 1: *K15, k2tog, rep from * 3 times more. (60 sts)
Rounds 2, 4: Knit.
Round 3: *K14, k2tog, rep from * 3 times more. (52 sts)

Row 2: K1, k2tog tbl, k7, k2tog, k1. (11 sts)
Continue as for Back of Ear until 5 sts rem (photo C).
BO.

5 WS facing each other, sew one Back of Ear to
one Front of Ear. Repeat for second Ear. Slide
the Monitor Cozy Mane onto your monitor and sew
Ears on at the upper corners.

6 **Optional Tail:**
Using dpns and D, CO 3 sts. Work I-cord as for
Mouse Tail for 20" (50cm). Divide sts onto three dpns
and beg working in rounds.
Join in A, B, and C, holding them tog with D as for
Mane.
Next Round: Knit around, inc into first st on each
needle by knitting into front and back of st.
Next Round: Knit.
Rep last 2 rounds until there are 15 sts total.
Work 3 rounds even.
Next Round: Knit around, knitting first 2 sts of each
needle tog.
Next Round: Knit.
Rep last 2 rounds until 3 sts rem.
Break yarn and thread through rem sts.
Sew Tail to either lower back corner of Mane.
Weave in ends.

Round 5: *K13, k2tog, rep from * 3 times more.
(44 sts)
BO all sts.

◤ MAKING THE MONITOR COZY EARS ◢

3 **Back of Ear (make 2):** Using straight ndls and
D, CO 15 sts.
Row 1: Purl.
Row 2: K1, k2tog tbl, k9, k2tog, k1. (13 sts)
Rep Rows 1-2, dec at each end of RS (even) rows as
before, until 5 sts rem.
BO (photo B).

4 **Front of Ear (make 2):** Using straight ndls
and holding D and E tog as one yarn, CO 13 sts.
Row 1: Purl.

TIPS | DIY Network Crafts

Making a Needle Chart
Does keeping track of what needles you
already have in your stash make your head
spin? Then make a paper needle chart that
fits in your wallet. Using a needle gauge, trace
circles for the various needle sizes onto the
card, and use a different colored card for each
needle type. Just fill in the circles for the ones
you already have and you'll always know what
you need and what you already have.

You'll make five ribbed cable blocks, and two each of the brioche bi-color and diamond brocade blocks. The best thing about a multi-block project is that once you knit the first one, the others are a snap. In addition to the written instructions, each of the pattern stitches have a chart for you to follow. When you're finished knitting and blocking, you'll single-crochet around each block before seaming them all together.

Designed by **LILY CHIN**

9-PATCH BABY BLANKET

This nine-patch blanket is great for babies, or as an elegant "lapghan" for your home. Our designer demonstrates two of her signature stitches—reversible cables and a bi-colored brioche stitch. What makes them unique is that they're just as neat on the backside as they are on the front.

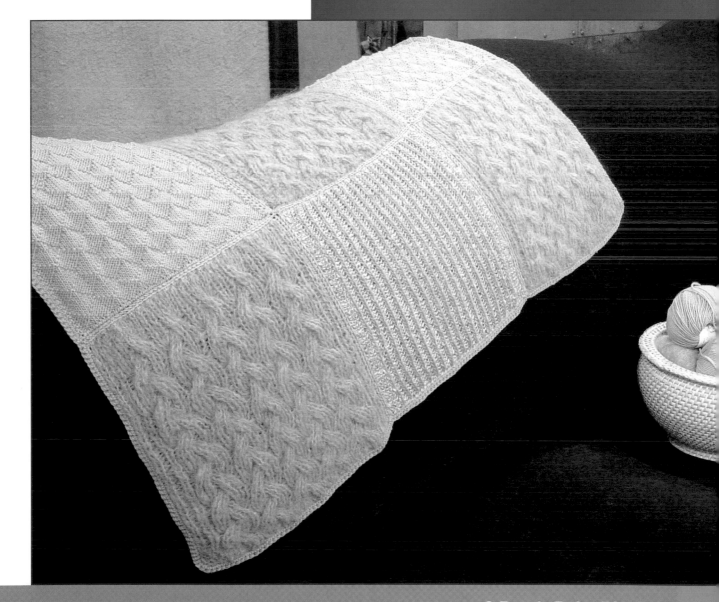

You Will Need

Approx 460 yds/420m of a bulky-weight mohair/wool-blend yarn in tan (A)

Approx 508 yds/464m of a light-weight wool yarn in tan (B)

Approx 138 yds/126m each of a medium-weight acrylic/mohair-blend yarn in ecru (C) and tan (D)

1 pair needles in size 9 U.S. (5.5mm)

1 pair needles in size 7 U.S. (4.5mm)

1 pair needles in size 5 U.S. (3.75mm)

1 circular needle in size 5 U.S. (3.75mm), any length, or set of same size dpns

Crochet hook, size E/4 (3.5mm)

Crochet hook, size H/8 (5mm)

Cable needle

Stitch markers

Tapestry needle

Extras

Gauges

For Reversibly Cabled Braid Block, each 12-st Braid = 2" (5cm) with largest needles

For Bi-colored Brioche Rib Block, 14 sts = 4" (10cm) with circular needle

For Diamond Brocade Block, 8-st Diamond = 1.5" (3.75cm) with smallest needle

Finished measurements

Approx 34" x 34" (85cm)

Note

When following Charts for Blocks, beg each row of Chart where indicated by arrows, and follow across row in direction indicated.

Special Abbreviations

4/4 Ribbed RC Cable: Place next 4 sts onto cable needle and hold to back of work, rib the next 4 sts from regular needle, then rib the 4 sts from cable needle.

4/4 Ribbed LC Cable: Place next 4 sts onto cable needle and hold to front of work, rib the next 4 sts from regular needle, then rib the 4 sts from cable needle.

◢ CASTING ON WITH THE CHAIN METHOD ◣

1 Make a slip knot around crochet hook, using hook indicated for each Block. Using needle size indicated for given Block, hold needle to the left of crochet hook, above working yarn. Working over the needle, catch working yarn with hook, and draw yarn loop over needle and through the slip knot loop on hook (photo A).

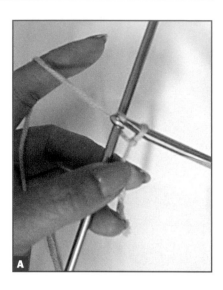
A

2 Slide work to tip of needle. Using crochet hook, slip new loop just made onto needle. (One stitch made). Slide st back to center of needle.

Rep Steps 1 and 2 until desired number of sts are cast on. Set crochet hook aside.

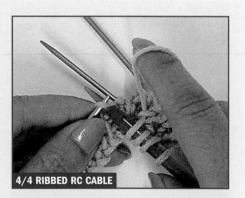
4/4 RIBBED RC CABLE

4/4 RIBBED LC CABLE

■ **MAKING THE REVERSIBLY CABLED BRAID BLOCKS** ■

3 NOTE: Slip the first st of every row as if to knit. (Make 5)

With larger hook and A, CO 68 sts using the chain method over medium-size needle.

Set up Ribbing: Slip first st, *p1, k1, rep from * to last st, p1.

Rep Row 1 until ribbing section meas approx ¾" (1.9cm), end with a WS row.

4 **Begin Braid Cable section** (illustration A): Change to largest needles.

Row 1 (RS): Slip first st, p1, k1, p1, (work 12-st rep of Row 1 of Reversibly Cabled Braid Block Chart) 5 times, k1, p1, k1, p1.

Row 2 (WS): Slip first st, p1, k1, p1, (work 12-st rep of Row 2 of Reversibly Cabled Braid Block Chart) 5 times, k1, p1, k1, p1.

Illustration A: Reversibly Cabled Braid Block

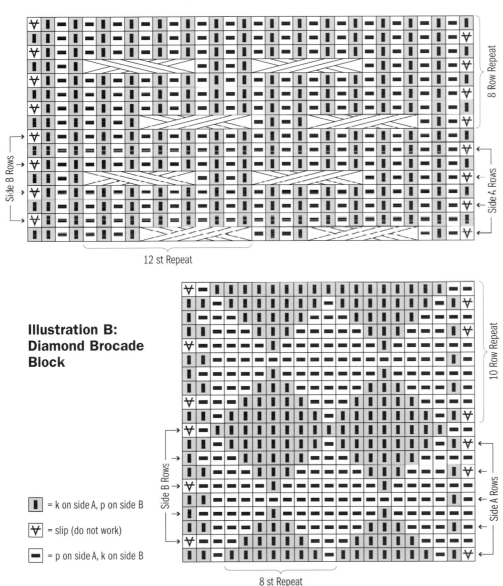

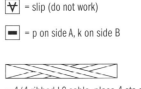

■ = k on side A, p on side B

⋎ = slip (do not work)

━ = p on side A, k on side B

= 4/4 ribbed LC cable, place 4 sts onto cable needle and hold in front of work, rib the next 4 sts from regular needle, then rib the 4 sts from cable needle

= 4/4 ribbed RC cable, place 4 sts onto cable needle and hold in back of work, rib the next 4 sts from regular needle, then rib the 4 sts from cable needle

8 Row Repeat

Side B Rows

Side A Rows

12 st Repeat

Illustration B: Diamond Brocade Block

10 Row Repeat

Side B Rows

Side A Rows

■ = k on side A, p on side B

⋎ = slip (do not work)

━ = p on side A, k on side B

8 st Repeat

Continue in this manner, keeping 4 sts at each edge in Ribbing, through Chart Row 8, then rep these 8 rows until Block meas approx 11¼" (28cm), ending with a WS row.

Change to medium needles and rep Row 1 of Ribbing section until top Ribbing meas approx ¾" (1.9cm), ending with a WS row. BO all sts.

◖ MAKING THE DIAMOND BROCADE BLOCKS ◗

5 NOTE: Slip the first st of every row as if to purl, with yarn in front of work.

(Make 2)

With smaller hook and B, CO 61 sts using the chain method over smallest size needle.

Set up Chart pattern (illustration B):

Row 1 (RS): Slip the first st as if to purl with yarn in front, k1, p1, k7, work (8-st rep of Row 1 of Diamond Brocade Block Chart) 6 times, p1, k2.

Row 2 (WS): Slip the first st as if to purl with yarn in front, k2, work (8-st rep of Row 2 of Diamond Brocade Block Chart) 6 times, k1, p5, k4.

Continue in this manner, work through Chart Row 10, then rep these 10 rows until Block meas approx 12" (30cm), ending with a WS row. BO all sts.

◖ MAKING THE BI-COLORED BRIOCHE RIB BLOCKS ◗

6 NOTES: Circular ndl or dpns must be used for this Block in order to slide sts to opposite end of needle without turning on many rows.

It takes two full passes across each row of sts to complete one row of knitting. For ease in following instructions, each pass across is called a separate Row.

(Make 2)

With larger hook and C, CO 44 sts using the chain method over smallest size needle (illustration C).

Foundation Row (RS):

With D, k3, pm, *k1, p1, rep from * across to last 3 sts, pm, k3. Do not turn. Slide sts to opposite end of needle.

Row 1 (RS): With C, p3, *k1, p1 into the st in the row below next st, rep from * to last 3 sts, p3. Turn.

Row 2 (WS): With D, p3, *k1, purl into the st in the row below next st, rep from * to last 3 sts, p3. Do not turn. Slide sts to opposite end of needle.

Row 3 (WS): With C, k3, *k1 into the st in the row below next st, p1, rep from * to last 3 sts, k3. Turn.

Row 4 (RS): With D, k3, *k1 into the st in the row below next st, p1, rep from * to last 3 sts, k3. Do not turn. Slide sts to opposite end of needle.

Rep Rows 1-4 until Block meas approx 12" (30cm). BO all sts very, very loosely, working all sts in patterns as established.

◖ FINISHING THE 9-PATCH BLANKET ◗

7 Weave in ends.
Block all pieces to measurements.

For each Block, using same size crochet hook as was used for CO for that Block, join yarn with a slip

Illustration C: Bi-Colored Brioche Rib Block

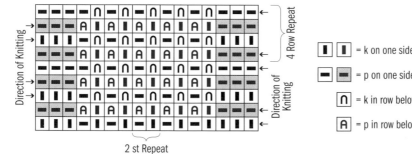

I **I** = k on one side, p on other side in either color A or color B

— **—** = p on one side, k on other side in either color A or color B

∩ = k in row below on one side, p in row below on other side with color B

A = p in row below on one side, k in row below on other side with color A

8 Sew Blocks tog by going through the front loop on the right-hand Block and then the back loop on the left-hand Block (photo B), following Arrangement of Blocks diagram for placement (illustration D).

Block finished Blanket one more time.

Illustration D: Arrangement of Blocks

A = Reversibly Cabled Braid Block

B = Diamond Brocade Cabled Braid Block

C = Bicolored Briche Rib Block

A	C	A
B	A	B
A	C	A

st into any corner of Block. Ch1, work one round of single crochet evenly spaced around entire edge of Block, working 3 sc into each corner. Join with a slip st into first sc. Cut yarn and fasten off.

Appendix
DYEING YOUR OWN YARN!

Yarn dyeing can be more than just a lot of fun—it can give you the feeling of being a color design wizard! In this section we show you how to dye your natural-colored yarns in three ways: immersion dyeing, resist immersion dyeing, and variegated dyeing. The process requires care and attention, but is really quite simple. The drying skeins look wonderful even before you knit them up! Once you've tried these methods, you'll want to experiment with new and different dye types, processes, and colorways. Have fun!

You Will Need

- Prewashed yarn in skein form, pre-soaked in water
- Cushing dye
- White vinegar
- Enamel or stainless steel (non-reactive) dyepot
- Heat source
- Apron
- Wet sponge for cleaning up spills
- Rubber gloves
- Tongs

- Dust mask
- pH strips (available at many retail and drugstore outlets)
- Water softener (optional)
- Garbage bags (for immersion dyeing with resists)
- Cotton strings (for immersion dyeing with resists)
- Glass casserole dish (for variegated yarn dyeing)
- Plastic cups (for variegated yarn dyeing)
- Syringe and/or Squeeze bottle (for variegated yarn dyeing)

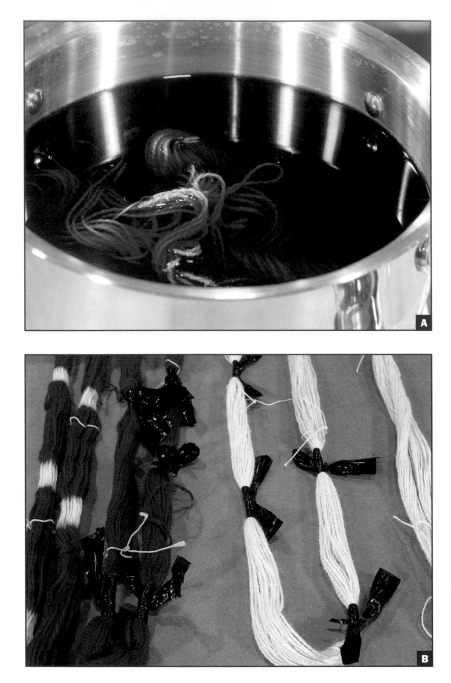

2 Fill the dyepot with water, making sure your dyepot is big enough for your yarn to move freely inside the dyebath. If the pot is not large enough, the yarn will not dye evenly. Add one cup of common white vinegar per pound of fiber. This makes the dyebath acidic. If your water is hard, fabric softener can aid the dyeing process by allowing better penetration of the dye into the fiber. Finally, add the dye solution to the dyebath and stir thoroughly.

3 Add the prewashed and presoaked yarn to the dyebath and begin to heat. Stir continuously as the water comes to a boil. Reduce heat and simmer for 30-40 minutes (photo A). As the color is taken up into the fiber, the dyebath will gradually become clearer. Different colors absorb at different rates. For example, blue "takes up" faster, and at lower temperatures, than yellow. So a green dye, made up of blue and yellow, will start out by turning the fiber mostly blue. The yellow will develop later, creating green.

If yarn is removed prematurely, uneven or off-shade dyeing (in the above case, excessively blue) may result. It is important to let the dyebath simmer until take-up is complete.

◀ IMMERSION DYEING ▶

1 Start by dissolving the dye powder in a small amount of boiling water (not in the main dyepot), remembering to wear your dust mask. This is the dye solution. One pack of dye will color a pound of fiber to a medium shade. The dyebath will consist of water, vinegar, water softener (if you have hard water), and the dye solution you've just made.

4 After the dyebath liquid is clear, remove the pot from the heat. Allow contents of dyebath to return to room temperature. Rinse the yarn well in cold water and hang from a hook to dry. You might wish to hang the yarn outside if the day is warm to speed up this process and air out the yarn at the same time.

◣ RESIST DYEING ◢

1 Prepare yarn and dyebath as for Immersion Dyeing. When yarn is ready, lay it on a clean countertop. Here, we will show you two ways to create "resists"—these are areas which the dye is prevented from penetrating.

2 Cut a plastic garbage bag into 12" (30cm) strips about 1" (2.5cm) wide. You may make the width larger if you wish more area to be covered. Wrap these strips tightly at various intervals around the yarn (photos B). Secure with an overhand knot. Dye the yarn as for Immersion Dyeing. Rinse well and hang to dry. When dry, remove the plastic strips to reveal the original yarn color underneath.

3 **Plastic Tie Alternative:** Take a strong cotton string and wrap it tightly around your prepared skein of yarn. This is similar to the techniques used in T-shirt tie-dyeing. There is no "right" way to do this; just have fun! You want to make sure that the string is tied very snugly, so that the dye will not penetrate the area under the string (photo C). Dye the yarn as for immersion dyeing. Rinse well and hang to dry. When dry, remove the strings to reveal light bands of the original yarn color amid the dyed areas.

◣ VARIEGATED DYEING ◢

Variegated yarn is much beloved by knitters everywhere for its fascinating and never-boring sequences of colors. The process of getting many different colors into the same skein of yarn often sports a name as colorful as the yarn itself, such as rainbow dyeing, tie-dyeing, sprinkle dyeing, and casserole dyeing. Our recipe uses Cushing dyes and will work on unspun fiber, yarn or cloth (whether used as material or ready-made clothing.) The only thing that matters here is that the fiber content be animal based, like silk, wool, camel, alpaca, angora, or mohair, and not synthetic or cotton.

1 Soak the fiber to be dyed in a vinegar water bath with a pH of 4.5 to 5.0. It will take about a tablespoon of vinegar per quart of water, but since

DYEING SAFETY

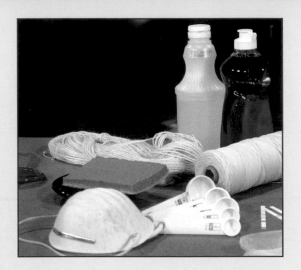

1. Use equipment only for dyeing and do not use same equipment for food.

2. Wear old clothes and an apron or smock.

3. Use gloves and a dust mask when you are mixing powdered chemicals and dyes.

4. Wipe up spills immediately with a damp paper towel and throw away.

5. Do not eat or drink while you work with dyes.

6. Use non-reactive plastic cups, bucket, spoons, etc., and stainless or enamel pots.

7. Work in a well-ventilated area; do not work with dyes in the kitchen or other enclosed space

water acidity varies, check with pH paper to be sure. Adjust if necessary.

2 For a medium shade, mix ¼ teaspoon of dye in ½ cup of water. Use more dye for darker shades and less for lighter shades. Mix as many colors as you like.

3 Remove fiber from the vinegar soak and gently squeeze out excess water. Lay fiber in a non-reactive baking pan—do not use aluminum, copper, or steel pans for this (photo D, previous page). Arrange the fiber as you like. You can fold, tie, twist, spiral or zigzag—whatever strikes your coloring fancy! Apply the dye with a squeeze bottle, sponge brush, or syringe (photo E, previous page)—or simply pour it directly on your chosen area of fiber. Remove any excess dye from the pan with a syringe.

4 After dyeing, the yarn will need to be heated to about 220 degrees Fahrenheit for one hour. Carefully put the yarn into a black plastic bag and place the bag in the sun for a couple of hours (photo F). You can also place the yarn in a slow cooker and leave overnight (but remember not to use any of your dyeing pots for cooking later!)

5 Rinse out excess dye from the yarn or fiber and wash fiber with a mild soap. Rinse well once more and hang to dry.

F

Index